# Diary of a Baby

OTHER BOOKS BY DANIEL STERN

*The First Relationship (1977)*
*The Interpersonal World of the Infant (1985)*

# DIARY OF
# A BABY

Daniel N. Stern, M.D.

**BasicBooks**
*A Division of* HarperCollins*Publishers*

Library of Congress Cataloging-in-Publication Data
Stern, Daniel N.
    Diary of a Baby / Daniel N. Stern.
        p.    cm.
    Includes bibliographical references and index.
    ISBN 0–465–01642–1 : $18.95
        1. Infant psychology—Case Studies. 2. Child psychology—Case
    studies.   I. Title.
    BF719.S74 1990                                          90–80241
    155.42'2—dc20                                               CIP

*This book is dedicated to my wife,*
*Nadia.*

# Contents

# CONTENTS

. . . also partly because it struck me, on my walk yesterday, that these moments of being of mine were scaffolding in the background: were the invisible and silent parts of my life as a child.

—Virginia Woolf

# Introduction
*～♁～*
## The Unfolding Worlds
## of a Baby's Life

*T*HIS book is the personal diary of a baby named Joey.
It is a diary I have invented to answer questions we all pose
about a baby's inner life. What is going on in your baby's
mind when she's gazing at your face, or looking at something as simple as a patch of sunshine on the wall or the bars
of her crib? How does your baby feel when he's hungry?
When he's sad? When he's fed? When you're playing face
to face? How does he feel when he's separated from you?

I have been pondering these questions and evolving answers to them for more than twenty years. I have spent
much of this time with babies. As a father, I have lived with
five of them. As an "infant psychiatrist," I have treated their
relationships with their parents. And as a researcher of development, I have observed and studied them.

At first, I saw infant experience as posing an intellectual
problem to be solved. But gradually I came to realize that
my interest stemmed from more than mere curiosity. I was

1

being drawn into a search for beginnings, into the very nature of human nature. We all were babies once. And we all have assumptions about babyhood and particular babies. None of us can be with a baby, care for a baby, or study a baby without ascribing to him or her certain thoughts, feelings, and wants at any particular moment. In a baby's presence, we are forced to invent that baby's inner worlds.

Indeed, the pervasiveness of our need to imagine an inner life for a baby became clear to me as I observed parents and their babies. I listened to their ordinary chatter, the things we all say to a baby almost without thinking: "Oh! you like that, huh?" "You don't want the green one, after all." "O.K., you're in a big rush, aren't you? I'll hurry up." "All better now, isn't it?" It is through such interpretations that parents know what to do next, and how to feel, what to think. Parenting itself depends on these interpretations. So do research and clinical practice and, in fact, the whole of a child's eventual development.

Most parents need and want to know what is going on inside a baby's head at certain moments—when she is hungry, say, or stares fixedly into the distance, or suddenly fusses in the middle of playing a game. At such times, parents try to slip beneath the baby's skin and into her mind and act as if they have a fair idea of what is going on there. And when they cannot identify their baby's experience, they simply make their best guess—a guess inevitably colored by how they themselves see the world. If, for example, you read anger in your baby's cry, you are likely to react with anger or guilt yourself. If you read only distress, you are likely to be able to feel, and to express, empathy easily and directly. Much of your response will depend on how you yourself were treated as a child—that is, on your parents' interpretation of your feelings and behavior.

These necessary guesses, or interpretations, of a baby's experience are usually positive and helpful. When you love someone, you want to share what it feels like to be that person. Indeed, it is here that intimacy and empathy start. Imagining what a baby is feeling is also a necessity for both you and the baby. Suppose she is about to cry, or looks at your nose and bursts into a smile. What do you do? You guess the baby's motives, wishes, and feelings from her expression and in terms of what has just been going on between the two of you: that is, your imagination, working upon your baby's behavior, comes up with an interpretation. This interpretation will both be your main guide in what you do next with your baby, and help her to learn about her own experience. She may not know exactly what she feels, or where she feels it, or just what she wants, or what is upsetting her. Her wishes, motives, feelings are relatively undefined. It is your interpretation that helps her to define them, to structure her world.

Indeed, parents of necessity keep a running record of how they imagine their baby is feeling and responding. They compose for their baby an ongoing biography, which they constantly consult. Thus, this biography serves as framework and dictionary for both how they see their baby and how she sees herself—and, hence, for her life.

In my clinical practice, I see striking evidence not only of the power of such parental constructions to affect a child, but of the strength of the parents' need to invent a child's inner experience. The more important of these constructions may be relatively remote in reference: "He is just like his grandfather, strong and quiet." "She is so like my mother who died, she has that same manner." "He will be rich and famous one day, and the destiny of our family will finally change." Or they may be closer to home: "She is so active and alert to everything, not at all like me." "I hope he won't be as fearful as I was." "He has his father's charm." These stories, created out of a parent's own past and present, reflect deep wishes, fears, and aspirations. Everyone creates such constructions, though psychological problems may arise when a parent's fantasy of who a child is, and what that child experiences, are contradictory.

Families, too, help to construct personal experience. Most babies become members of the families they are born into, and each family has particular rules for interpreting personal experience. In some, feeling anger is bad; in others, it is acceptable, even potentially good; and yet in others, anger is not even allowed to exist, is not recognized as a "legitimate" experience. The baby discovers these rules, in part, when her own experience is interpreted only in certain ways and not in others. Each infant's inner life is thus shaped differently.

Of course, society, too, has certain assumptions whereby it interprets and shapes the experience of its members through schools and other institutions. For example, clinical theories of developmental changes—such as Freud's or Margaret Mahler's or Erik Erikson's—are inspired by and founded upon hidden or unstated fantasies about the nature of infant experience. The same is true of infant research, where experiments and observations are often directed, implicitly, by the imagined inner life we attribute to infants.

Thus, parents and psychologists—as well as everyone else involved with children—build for the child a sort of biography. In inventing this diary for a baby named Joey, I am

I am taking the process one step further to create a sort of autobiography. I have devised it not only to enlighten parents about the inner life of their babies but as a research strategy, which has led to hypotheses about infant perception, emotion, and memory, and about how a baby experiences his own development, his own past.

By no means did I construct this diary out of whole cloth. Its "cloth" is part speculation, part imagination, part fact—all emerging from our current knowledge of infants. Over the past decades, there has been a revolution in the scientific observation of babies; in fact, we have more systematic observations on the first two years of life than on any other period in the entire life span.

This revolution turned, in part, on our learning to ask babies questions they could actually answer. Once good potential answers were discovered, good questions could be asked. For instance, one good potential answer is turning the head to one side or another—something even a newborn can do voluntarily. A good question is, Can a two-day-old baby know his own mother by her smell? The question and the potential answer got yoked as follows. A breast pad wet from the nursing mother was put on the pillow on the right side of the head of a baby several days old. A second wet breast pad, brought from another mother, was placed on the left side of his head. The infant turned his head to the right. When the pads were reversed, he turned to the left. He not only knew his own mother's smell, he preferred it, and he answered by turning his head.

Another good potential answer is sucking. Infants are, of course, good suckers. All infants suck in short bursts, then pause for a moment, then begin another burst, and so on. They can control the length of the bursts or pauses. To answer the question What do babies like to look at? we can place an electronically bugged nipple into a baby's mouth and hook it up to a slide projector so that the baby can see the projection. A baby of three months or so quickly learns that each time she wants to see a new picture, she need only start to suck; and when she wants just to look at it, she pauses. The baby will turn over the slides at the rate that reflects her interest in each picture. From such an experiment, using well-designed pictures, infants' visual preferences can be explored and mapped.

Or, the bugged nipple can be hooked up to two audiocassette machines. One has a recording of the mother's voice; the other, the voice of another woman saying the same thing. In this setup, the baby will suck so that he can spend more time listening to his own mother's voice, thus answering the question whether he recognizes it. There are other potential baby answers to the myriad of questions we want to ask: gazing, eye movements, heart rate, leg kicks, and so on. And all are used in research today.

Television also revolutionized our ability to make fine observations of infants and parents together. Now we can freeze a frame, review a gesture or facial expression many times over, measure its duration exactly. As a research tool for exploring human behavior—especially nonverbal interactions—the television camera has been as important as the microscope was in revealing hitherto unseen organisms.

So far as possible, I have based Joey's diary on current knowledge about infants. Some of this information has come from my own research; most, from researchers and observers around the world. At the end of this book is a highly selective bibliography of the principal research findings that inspired it.

The structure of this diary is based on the discontinuous leaps that occur in a baby's development. Each leap brings a baby forward into a more complex world of experience. To show how a baby is likely to live the unfolding of these successive worlds, I have Joey chart his progress through five successive worlds of experience: from early babyhood to the point when at four years he is ready to step forward and create his own story. Thus, at six weeks, Joey is in the first of his worlds, the World of Feelings, where the inner feeling tone of an experience anchors his impressions. Here he is concerned not with how or why something has happened, but with the actual, raw experience itself; not with facts or things, but with feelings, *his* feelings. At four months, he passes into the Immediate Social World. In this world of the "here and now, between us," he reports on the rich choreography between himself and his mother, on the subtle moves by which they regulate their flow of feelings. Thus, Joey introduces us to the basic dance we all play out with other people throughout our lives.

At twelve months, Joey discovers that he has a mind, and that other people do, too. In the World of Mindscapes, he becomes aware of such internal mental events as wishes and intentions. He finds that one person's mental landscape can overlap with another's: one may have the same thing in mind, or not. For instance, he comes to know both that his mother knows that he wants a cookie, and that she knows that he knows.

Over half a year later, at twenty months, Joey takes us into the World of Words, with its paradoxical combination of advantages and disadvantages. Here he discovers that sound symbols can both throw open new vistas of imagination and communication and, at the same time, create havoc with his old nonverbal worlds.

Finally, there is the big leap to four years, when Joey is finally able to talk about himself in his own voice. Now he has the abilities to think about and make sense of his experiences, and then to construct an autobiographical story about them to relate to someone else. He has entered the World of Stories.

In his diary, Joey touches on a wide range of events and common experiences every parent will recognize: some casual, like looking at the bars of his crib; some crucial, like being hungry. A few moments of experience at each age can show the drama and effect of the most ordinary as well as the extraordinary moments in a baby's development. Each moment is rich in implication, a world in a grain of sand.

Most diaries are, of necessity, records of events in the past. In Joey's diary, however, everything occurs in the present. Events run directly from his experience of them into the diary without any delay and without the reconstruction an adult would find necessary to "fix the present." The events that occur in Joey's diary are like dreams being filmed.

Of course, babies do not have words. They cannot write, speak, even think with words. Thus, Joey's voice is one I created for him. To capture the essence of his nonverbal experiences, I have borrowed freely from sounds, images, weather, space, movement. As Joey gets older, and more able to differentiate his experience, the descriptions in his diary entries become more detailed. As his memory gets better, the descriptions become longer and contain more parts.

Though I have to use language for Joey's voice, I have

tried to make that language reflect aspects of his worldview. For instance, when Joey is six weeks old, he does not use personal pronouns—*I, me, her*—because he cannot yet differentiate between himself and his mother or any other caregiver. Similarly, such temporal words as *then* or *after* appear only when Joey has some notion of how events follow one another. And conjunctions like *because* occur only when he has a substantial sense of causality.

Each of the parts in this book covers one of the successively unfolding worlds in a baby's life: the World of Feelings, the Immediate Social World, the World of Mindscapes, the World of Words, and the World of Stories. At the beginning of each part, I introduce the new abilities and capacities available to Joey at the particular age that make up that new world of experience. The chapters within each part center on an event that occurs in the course of an ordinary morning. We see that event from three points of view: first, a brief setting to give the context of the event; then Joey's diary account of it in the voice I have created for him; and, finally, my comments on Joey's experience in the light of our knowledge of infancy.

Repeating the same event at a different age—for instance, Joey's response to a patch of sunlight when he is six weeks old and again when he is twenty months—allows me to highlight the developmental changes that occur in a baby between the World of Feelings and that of Words. In the final chapter (the only one where Joey speaks in his actual voice), many of these same moments reappear but transformed into his own story.

As he matures, Joey encounters each world in succession. Yet he never fully leaves behind the previous worlds. Nor does each new world replace those worlds; it adds something to them. So when Joey enters the Immediate Social World, it does not push aside or totally absorb the World of Feelings but adds another note. And, as in music, when a second note is added to the first, both sound different in the presence of each other. In this fashion, as each new world is added to the existing worlds, it alters them.

We live in all of these worlds at the same time. They overlap, but never disappear. Out of the interplay between them arises the richness of human experience, a dynamic most clearly seen in the World of Stories. Thus, *Diary of a Baby* records a journey through worlds that, unfolding for each human being early in life, endure for a lifetime.

# THE WORLD OF FEELINGS: JOEY AT SIX WEEKS

STEP into Joey's earliest world and recall what you have never really forgotten. Imagine that none of the things you see or touch or hear have names or functions, and few any memories attached to them. Joey experiences objects and events mainly in terms of the *feelings* they evoke in him. He does not experience them as objects in and of themselves, or for what they do or are called. When his parents call him "honey," he doesn't know that *honey* is a word and refers to him. He doesn't even particularly notice it as a sound distinct from a touch or a light. But he attends carefully to how the sound flows over him. He feels its glide, smooth and easy, soothing him; or its friction, turbulent and stirring him up, making him more alert. Every experience is like that, having its own special feeling tone—for infants as for adults. But we pay less attention to it. Our sense of being is not focused on it as Joey's is.

Now, pretend that weather is the only medium. Pretend

that chairs, walls, light, and people all make up a weatherscape, a special moment of a day or night, its unique mood
and force deriving from its own combination of wind,
light, and temperature. And pretend that there are no objects
for the weather to affect, no trees to be blown, no field or
harbor for the rain to pelt. And, finally, that there is no you
to stand outside the weather and watch it happen. You are
part of the weatherscape. The prevailing mood and force
can come from inside you and shape or color everything
you see outside. Or, they can start outside and resonate
inside you. In fact, the distinction between inside and outside is still vague: both may seem to be part of a single
continuous space. As adults, we have many moments when
the inside and the outside worlds seem to influence one
another directly, almost flow freely one into the other. For
instance, the inside moves to the outside when someone
close to you does something hateful and looks for that
moment intensely ugly. Or, the outside moves inside when
you walk out into an unexpectedly sunny and clear morning, and your spirits lift and your body lightens. In adults,
these partial breaches in the inside-outside barrier are short-
lived. In infants, they are almost constant.

A human weatherscape is a unique moment of feelings-
in-motion. It is not static like a photograph. It has duration,
like a chord or several notes or even a musical phrase. It can
last from a split second to many seconds. And during the
time that fills a moment, Joey's feelings and perceptions
change together. Each moment has its own sequence of
feelings-in-motion: a sudden increase in interest; a rising,
then a falling wave of hunger pain; an ebbing of pleasure.
It is as a sequence of these moments strung together that
Joey experiences life.

The four chapters in part I describe four such moments as they occur one after the other on a single morning when Joey is six weeks old. In the first, Joey is looking at the sunlight falling on his wall ("A Patch of Sunshine"). Then he looks at the bars of his crib and, through them, at the wall beyond ("Space Songs"). He becomes hungry and cries ("A Hunger Storm") and, finally, is fed ("The Hunger Storm Passes"). Like shots in a movie, one moment may be continuous with the next, or fade into it, or cut abruptly against it, or be separated from it by a blank pause. It is not clear to Joey how he gets from one moment to the next or what, if anything, happens between them. (Is it so clear for us?) But all his senses are focused on each one, and he lives each intensely. Many are the prototypes of moments that will recur over and over throughout his life.

1

# A Patch of Sunshine:
# 7:05 A.M.

*J*OEY has just awakened. He stares at a patch of sunshine on the wall beside his crib.

— ❦ —

*A space glows over there,*
*A gentle magnet pulls to capture.*
*The space is growing warmer and coming to life.*
*Inside it, forces start to turn around one another in a slow*
*    dance.*
*The dance comes closer and closer.*
*Everything rises to meet it.*
*It keeps coming. But it never arrives.*
*The thrill ebbs away.*

— ❦ —

For Joey, most encounters with the world are dramatic and emotional—a drama whose elements and nature are not obvious to us as adults. Of all the things in the room, it is the patch of sunshine that attracts and holds Joey's attention. Its brightness and intensity are captivating. At six weeks of age, he can see quite well, though not yet perfectly. He is already aware of different colors, shapes, and intensities. And he has been born with strong preferences about what he wants to look at, about what pleases him. Among these preferences, intensity tops the list. It is the most important element in this scene. A baby's nervous system is prepared to evaluate immediately the intensity of a light, a sound, a touch—of anything accessible to one of his senses. How intensely he feels about something is probably the first clue he has available to tell him whether to approach it or to stay away. Intensity can lead him to try to protect himself. It can guide his attention and curiosity and determine his internal level of arousal. If something is only mildly intense (like a lamp lit in daylight), his attraction to it is weak. If too intense (like direct sunlight), he avoids it. But if it is moderately intense, like the patch of sunshine, he is spellbound. That just-tolerable intensity arouses him. He immediately alters in response to it. It increases his animation, activates his whole being. His attention is sharper. The patch of sunshine is a "gentle magnet," whose force he feels.

At this age, Joey is also drawn to areas enclosed in a clearly marked frame. The edges of the square sunpatch catch his eye at the line where lighter and darker wall meet. In a sense, the sunlight pulls, and the edges capture.

How does Joey know that the glowing space is "over there"? How does he know that it is not, for example, "over here," close at hand? Even at this young age, Joey is able to calculate distances and quadrants of space. Soon he will divide all space into two distinct areas: a near world within the reach of his extended arm, and a far world beyond it. Not for another few months will Joey be able to reach for, and grasp, what he wants with precision. Nonetheless, he is preparing at six weeks to distinguish between reachable and nonreachable space in this way. (This ability will help him learn the crucial act of reaching by defining for him which things are actually within reach. It would not be useful if he tried to reach for the moon—or even for things far across the room.) His space is not continuous and seamless like an adult's. It is as though a bubble were to form around him at the radius of his arm's length. Even blind babies, when starting to reach, reach for a sound-making object only when it comes within that radius. They carve up distance the same way as the sighted babies do, but with their ears, not their eyes. Thus the sunpatch, being beyond Joey's future reach, is "over there."

Why does the sunpatch "come to life" for Joey and reveal to him forces that turn around one another in a slow dance? These effects depend on how Joey explores the sunpatch with his eyes and his attention. At this age, babies often stare at things as if their gaze has indeed been captured and they are obliged to stare at one spot. A baby in this state appears, as Joey does, to be active mentally—not lost in a vague reverie, as an adult would be.

Parents can feel challenged, even upset by such moments in a baby's life. Imagine holding your six-week-old baby girl in your arms. You're face to face. You want to play, but she is transfixed by a spot where your forehead and your hairline meet. You, wanting her to look into your eyes, smile at her to divert her gaze. But your smile is not successful. You may—as most parents do—go on trying to divert her. You may make silly faces or even shake your baby from side to side, hoping the physical movement will unhook her gaze. But she may well continue to gaze at your hairline. Many parents interpret this gaze aversion as real rejection and may even give up trying for the moment to make eye contact. This is not any kind of rejection, however, but a normal phenomenon. It has been called *obligatory attention.*

Now, sometimes you succeed in changing and capturing your baby's gaze; sometimes you don't. But even when you don't—even when she never lets go visually of your hairline, of the "edge" where it meets your forehead—you often get the impression she is taking in your antics in some way. And so she is. She is paying attention to your face, but peripherally. She is transfixed by the frame, not by the picture. And that's the point.

Joey is staring at the edge made by the square of light against the wall. But just because he is staring at one point on the edge of the sunpatch doesn't mean that he is paying attention only to that one spot. Although we are usually not aware of it, we can easily separate our *focus of vision* (exactly what our eyes are looking at) from our *focus of attention* (exactly what our mind is paying attention to). Think of driving a car. Your eyes are fixed on the road ahead, but your attention can wander from side to side (to objects in peripheral vision) or far away or into the past. Or, better, choose one spot on a blank white page and stare at it. When after a while the spot becomes boring, your focus of attention, but not your eyes, will start to wander outside the fixed spot to other areas just around it. As your attention hovers over these new areas, they appear to change, even to disappear. The colors may start to drift. What initially appeared all white has now a hint of green or red in it. And these two colors may flip-flop. Or, the brightness and shading of the areas may shift like a slow play of light falling on a hillside through drifting clouds. Or, the flat page can appear to change its shape around the spot: it can buckle or melt or curve away. Such illusions occur when our focal attention and our visual fixation separate and play off each other.

Joey, too, will soon get bored looking at the exact same spot at the edge of the sunpatch. Probably his focal vision gets stuck on one spot, while his focus of attention starts to wander away from it. He begins to explore, with his attention, the interior of the sunpatch which appears in his peripheral vision. And as soon as he does that, he experiences illusions like an adult's. The patch of sunshine starts to "come alive" for him. It begins to move, to change color and shape. He does not know that these are just tricks played on the mind by the tension between vision and attention. For Joey, the patch of sunshine, in coming to life, reveals a play of forces. He sees dancing. He enters into a dynamic relationship with the patch of sunshine, each acting upon the other. All Joey's perceptions are like this. There are no "dead," inanimate objects out there. There are only different forces at play. As Joey engages with them, the sunpatch becomes dynamic and starts a slow turning dance.

The sunpatch appears to grow warmer and to keep coming closer as a result of the play of colors. Infants by this age have color vision. The patch of sunshine is, of course, yellowish against the white wall; the latter, by comparison, looks slightly bluish where the sun does not strike it. "Warm" intense colors, like yellow, appear to come forward; and "cooler" colors like blue, to recede and move back. So, to Joey, the sunshine patch appears to advance toward him, while the space immediately surrounding the patch appears to move away. The space has both a center that constantly approaches, like a note slowly rising higher, but never disappearing out of range; and a surrounding area that slowly recedes. This center, alive with the spectacle of dancing forces, appears to keep approaching him but never reaches him. Also, the advancing sunpatch against the re-treating wall appears to be continually turning inside out.

In this interaction with a sunpatch, Joey feels everything rising "to meet it," a sort of promise ("It keeps coming"), and finally an "ebbing" of the "thrill" of suspense. The play of illusions and feelings fascinates Joey. It is a light show that captures not only his eyes but his entire nervous system. Infants love experiences where stimulation and excitation mount—if not too fast or too high. (When you want to grab and hold your baby's attention, you intuitively jazz up your voice and facial expressions.) And they tend to get bored and move away from situations where the stimulation is low or stops changing. So, after a while, Joey gets bored by the play of appearances he sees in the sunpatch. Its infinite approach stops being new and suspenseful. His attention suddenly dies away, and he looks elsewhere for a different experience. At this point, he turns his head away from the sunlit wall.

# 2

*Space Songs:*

*7:07 A.M.*

$\mathcal{J}$OEY has just turned away from the sunlit wall and looks at the bars of his crib and past them to the darker far wall.

— ❧ —

*Suddenly a piece of space stands out.*
*It's a pillar, thin and taut.*
*It stands motionless and sings out a bright melody.*
*Now, from close by, different notes drift in.*
*There is nearby another pillar of space.*
*It, too, sings—but in harmony with the first.*
*The two melodies mingle in a tight duet,*
*one melody loud, the other quiet.*
*Far away, large, soft volumes now show themselves.*
*They beat out a slower, deeper rhythm.*
*The near, bright duet runs in and out of the far, slow*
  *rhythm.*

*The two spaces weave together into a single song that fills
the world.
Then, from somewhere else, sounds a different note.
A shooting star, it flashes past and quickly disappears.*

———— ❧ ————

As soon as Joey turns his head, he is confronted, even
affronted, by the dark, shiny crib bar closest to his face.
Whether it jumped there by itself, or appeared there only
when he turned his head to find it, is not yet a concern of
Joey's. He is aware of it—"suddenly"—in front of him and
in the close plane, not the far one.

This bar stands out as distinct from the shaded wall and
other spaces beyond. It is made of brightly varnished dark
wood. It easily captures his attention. First, because it is
close to him, it appears well defined, cleaner, tighter, more
vivid. At this age, Joey can only partially adjust the focus
of his eyes to accommodate objects at various distances.
Since he cannot yet see clearly across the room, the larger
areas of the far wall appear fuzzy, but still visible—as the
details of a distant landscape are blurred to adult eyes.

For Joey, the crib bar is not just a wooden object. It is
a special kind of volume standing amidst many other
volumes and spaces around him. But the crib bar has a
different feeling tone from the rest of that space. The term
*feeling tone* denotes the various feelings the crib bar might
evoke in one experiencing it not as a minor part of a piece
of nursery furniture but as an object in and of itself—as we
would experience, say, an abstract piece of sculpture. How
to imagine that?

In the parlor game of Botticelli, the person who is "it"
chooses in secret someone he is thinking of, and then says,

"I am thinking of a person." The other players try to guess who that person is by asking a special kind of question: "If the person were a piece of cloth, what would he feel like to touch?" "If she were a color, what color would she be?" "If he were a musical note, which one?" "If she were a song, who would have composed or played her?" "If he were a moment of the day, what hour would it be?" "If she were a temperature, a kind of weather, a taste, . . ." and so on.

To play the game, the players must share more than a knowledge of the person whose identity they will try to guess. They must be able to grasp certain qualities of experience: tension, hardness, softness, clarity, brightness, intensity, speed, roundness, sharpness. And they must be able to grasp these qualities from the exercise of any of the senses: vision, taste, touch, hearing, smell. Further, they must be able to translate the quality derived from one sensory modality—say, vision—and recognize it in any other—say, hearing. Some of the rich effects of poetry rest on this intuitive ability to translate between the senses, as in these lines from Baudelaire's *Correspondances* (1857):

> *There are odors fresh as the skin of an infant,*
> *Sweet as flutes, green as any grass,*
> *And others, corrupt, rich and triumphant.*

Infants are born with the capacity to play Botticelli. Their nervous systems are designed so that they can do this without prior experience. Of course, experience helps, too. For instance, a three-week-old baby who is blindfolded, and given a nipple of a new shape she has never touched or seen before, will suck on it to get the feel of it. When we remove it from her mouth and place it next to another nipple she

25

also has never before seen, and take the blindfold off, she will spend much more time looking at the nipple she has just sucked, so that we can infer that she now distinguishes and recognizes it from the other one. In other words, the baby is able to abstract from touch (by mouthing) the shape of the nipple and to transfer into the visual mode the knowledge of that shape. Thus, a baby comes to know what the sucked object should look like. The nipple has become visually "familiar."

Now to Joey, the crib bar has certain abstract qualities: straightness; an elongated, thin shape; bright highlights, where the varnish reflects the light; high density; sharpness of form or outline against a more diffuse background; and so on. As each of these abstract qualities evokes a feeling in Joey, the bar provides an emotional experience. Just as adults, in playing Botticelli with both their perceptions and their feelings, attempt to capture an "essential experience," so Joey does with the crib bar: if it were a song, it might sound like a cornet and an oboe in close, vivacious harmony. That is the "bright melody" the bar sings. These feeling tones that captivate Joey are no different from ours; only, we have the means and diversity of experiences by which to translate and express them.

"Now, from close by, different notes drift in." Joey is just starting to notice that there is more than one crib bar. He probably doesn't notice the next one right away; rather, its presence sneaks up on him. Seeing the first bar primes him to notice the second. It is like our common experience of encountering a new word, and then having it pop up surprisingly often in the next few days as though it were really not so unusual after all. Why this happens is not clear. But it is probably something like this: The first bar Joey sees (or the new word we hear) sets up specific patterns of activation, visual as well as emotional, that include the bar's feeling tone. While these new patterns remain activated, Joey is likely (as are we) to find something in the outside world that matches them. Thus, the threshold for noticing the second bar, compared with the other objects around him, has been lowered.

Joey then shifts his gaze to the next crib bar, and the first drama begins for him: the drama of evaluating whether two things are the same or not. The second bar creates a similar experience; it is singing a "similar but not identical song." Infants are naturally driven to explore whether experiences are identical, or similar (a variation), or totally unlike. Here Joey senses a difference between the bars, even though it is slight: distance, shading, angle of view, and so on. To him, the two bars are in harmony—in fact, in a "tight duet," "tight" because the two melodies are so much alike.

The bars can be in harmony only if Joey can keep both of them in mind at the same time. If he can't do that, he will "hear" one solo and then, a moment later when he switches gaze, a second, similar solo. But there will be no true duet. Until babies are three to four months old, they seem to focus their attention on only one thing at a time. And when they refocus their attention on a second object, they seem to forget about the first. It is enough "out of mind" that the baby does not search to make connections between the two. In most situations, then, Joey should experience no duets, not yet anyway. In a situation like this, however, where he is simply receiving sensory stimulation, I suspect that each sensory impression leaves a sort of afterglow in memory, so that the second impression is still, for a short while, bathed in the first. That is why the duet consists of "one melody loud, the other quiet." After all, he sees them simultaneously even when he is focusing on one.

The emerging interaction between foreground bars and background wall makes up the second drama for Joey. Both infants and adults see objects and space in terms of spatial frequency. For example, a picket fence has a certain number of units (fence posts) for each unit of the *visual field* (the panorama seen). The density of units makes up its *spatial frequency*. A group of three little boys spread unevenly in front of the picket fence will have a different spatial frequency. The picture of boys and fence is made of two spatial frequencies superimposed. As adults, we easily discriminate little boys from fence posts, or crib bars from walls and doors. And so does Joey. But he does it because the spatial frequency of the crib bars is faster (denser) and more regular than that of the background wall and door, not because of what they are as objects. The fact that the bars are closer also helps.

It is the contrast of spatial frequencies (fast and regular versus slow and irregular) and of qualities (taut, bright, and clean versus loose, diffuse, soft, and attenuated) that gives rise to both the near, bright song and the far, slower song, each existing in different planes of space. Relating the two songs, the two planes of space, is at the heart of the second drama. As Joey's attention flip-flops between foreground and background, the quick, regular, simple harmony of the crib bars is joined by the slow, loose rhythm of the far wall and door. Something creative must take place in Joey's apparently aimless alternation of gaze. The faster foreground can measure out in regular clean beats the fuzzy drift of the background. Or, the background with its broader cadence can hold and tie together several pieces of the foreground. Each reversal of focus makes the opposite one come more alive. When Joey focuses on one, he can still hear the echo or see the afterglow of the other. A close world and a far world are coming together, and the space surrounding Joey is slowly starting to become unified in his mind.

"Then, from somewhere else, sounds a different note. A shooting star, it flashes past and quickly disappears." At this age, Joey has little control over his arm movements. When he is intensely observing and aroused by what he sees, his arms may rapidly swing and jerk about purposelessly. At this moment, one of his arms has swung forward into his visual field and then quickly swung back and disappeared. All babies are extremely sensitive to things that move. In fact, their *peripheral vision* (what one sees at the side) is the most sensitive in picking up movement. *Central* (or foreal) *vision* is better at picking up form. This makes sense because as vigilant animals our safety and well-being depend on our being able to perceive movements outside our direct line of vision. When one perceives a movement at the periphery, one can then turn head and eyes exactly in that direction to see what has moved, and then decide whether to flee or chase.

The "different note" is Joey's own hand which, flying in and then out of his peripheral vision, has partially diverted his attention from the crib bars. He does not, of course, know that it is his hand. He perceives only a movement. This "shooting star" comes "from somewhere else"—that is, the periphery—and is different in speed and duration from what he has been watching.

Out of such perceptions, the infant constructs a unified world made up of many different kinds of events. The "different note" is the very beginning of another integration Joey will soon have to make: to know that the hand he sees moving is the same both as the one he feels to be moving, and as the one he intends to move.

Thus, a baby enters upon the huge task of making sense of different parts of the world, almost all at the same time.

# 3

# A Hunger Storm:
# 7:20 A.M.

I T is four hours since Joey's last feeding, and he is probably hungry. Suddenly his lower lip protrudes. He starts to fret. Soon the fretting gives way to jerky crying, then moves into a full cry.

*A storm threatens. The light turns metallic. The march of clouds across the sky breaks apart. Pieces of sky fly off in different directions. The wind picks up force, in silence. There are rushing sounds, but no motion. The wind and its sound have separated. Each chases after its lost partner in fits and starts. The world is disintegrating. Something is about to happen.*

*Uneasiness grows. It spreads from the center and turns into pain.*

*It is at the center that the storm breaks out. It is at the very center that it grows stronger and turns into pulsing waves. These waves push the pain out, then pull it back again.*

*The wind and the sounds and the pieces of sky are all pulled back into the center. There they find one another again, are reunited. Only to be thrown outward and away, then sucked back in to form the next wave—darker and stronger.*

*The pulsing waves swell to dominate the whole weatherscape. The world is howling. Everything explodes and is blown out and then collapses and rushes back toward a knot of agony that cannot last—but does.*

—— ❧ ——

Hunger is a powerful experience, a motivation, a drive. It sweeps through an infant's nervous system like a storm, disrupting whatever was going on before and temporarily disorganizing behavior and experience. Then it establishes its own patterns of action and feelings, its own rhythms.

The sensation of hunger begins weakly but grows rapidly. While it is still weak and inconstant, Joey probably experiences it as a general irritability that interrupts the smooth functioning of his entire self. Everything is affected—his movements, breathing, attention, feeling, arousal, perceptions, and so on. This "global" interference must feel to Joey like a sudden disharmony in his world, a "something going wrong." The feeling tone of everything must suddenly shift for him as happens before a storm when the "light turns metallic."

During this disorganizing phase as the hunger grows, the world must appear disjointed and fractured. With his attention pulled inward for moments at a time, he can view the world about him only in snatches. What he normally follows as one continuous evolving event now has gaps—just as if a scene had stopped suddenly and then continued at a different place or point in time. Thus is Joey's experience fractured: he jerks his arms and legs, shattering his weatherscape. "The march of clouds across the sky breaks apart. Pieces of sky fly off in different directions."

Most disorganizing of all is the change in his breathing. As Joey's hunger grows, it begins to superimpose its own order on the disorganization. First, it recruits Joey's respirations. He breathes faster, stronger, more jaggedly. Soon, his voice—the vocalizations that make the cry sound—comes into play. But while the hunger is building, Joey's breathing (the "wind") and his cry (the "sound") are not yet integrated. Sometimes he breathes without voicing. Sometimes short cries punctuate the end of an expiration but do not yet overlap its full length. Sometimes the crying expirations last too long and leave Joey out of breath.

This discoordination between breathing and crying is for Joey as if "the wind and its sound have separated. Each chases after its lost partner in fits and starts." Joey's sputtering sounds and jerky motions also make up this discoordinated phase of his distress. His arm and leg movements are not synchronized either with each other or with his crying and breathing. For Joey, the "world is disintegrating" reflects a profound disruption of ease, a diffuse feeling with no focus.

But finally, as his hunger grows, it starts to localize within him, somewhere that feels like "the center." (Joey doesn't know yet that it is *his* center; it is simply the center of the entire worldscape.) Two things happen. First, a clear sensation of hunger emerges from the background of irritability. "It is at the center that the storm breaks out." Second, the hunger pain pushes Joey's nervous system to shift gears. He eases into the powerful rhythm of a full-throated cry. These are the pulsing waves. Full-throated crying is not a state of disorganization at all. It is a separate and distinct organization of the central nervous system, a state that recoordinates Joey's behavior according to its own patterning.

The new order of the full cry consists of fast, deep, gulping inspirations of air (the pulling back into the center) and then long expirations accompanied with the loud cry that rides each expiration to its very end (the throwing back out and away). His breathing and voicing have finally been recoupled, and his world starts to reorganize. "The wind and the sounds and the pieces of sky are all pulled into the center. There they find one another again, are reunited. Only to be hurled outward and away."

As the full cry grows louder, it engulfs and coordinates all Joey's activities and experiences. The powerful expirations of this cry probably give Joey momentary relief from the pain—just as yelling and jumping up and down "relieve" a stubbed toe. He is now acting in a coordinated way, not just passively experiencing. Also, his efforts and the noise he makes help distract him. As he cries out, Joey feels as if he is hurling the pain sensation out and away, over and over again. And between breaths, the sensation intensifies anew inside. "These pulsing waves swell to dominate the whole weatherscape. Everything explodes and is blown out." Collapsing, it "rushes back toward a knot of agony."

Joey's organized full cry helps deal with the hunger in two ways. It is a beautifully designed signal (police and ambulance sirens have learned from it) to alert his parents to his distress and to demand a response from them. At the same time, it may help him modulate the intensity of the hunger sensation. Hunger, thus, creates in Joey ways of both reaching the outside world and coping with the one inside.

# 4

## The Hunger Storm Passes:
## 7:25 A.M.

*J*OEY'S mother, hearing his hunger cries, enters the room. She speaks to him in a soft, soothing voice. She picks him up and holds him against her chest with her left arm, while she unbuttons her blouse with her other hand, talking all the while. She then puts him to her breast. He finds the nipple and sucks avidly. After a while, he sucks more easily and looks at his mother's face.

———

*At once the world is enveloped. It becomes smaller and slower and more gentle. The envelope pushes away the vast empty spaces. Everything is shifting. A faint promise spurts. The pulsations of explosion and collapse are being tamed. But they are still there, still wild, still ready to break through.*

*Somewhere, between the boundary, and the very center of the storm, there is a tug, a pulling together. Two magnets wobble toward each other, then touch, lock tight.*

*At the point of contact, a new, fast rhythm begins. It rides on top of the slowly pulsing waves of the storm. This new rhythm is short and greedy. Everything strains to strengthen it. With each beat, a current flows to the center. The current warms the chill. It cools the fire. It loosens the knot at the center and saps the fierceness of the pulsations until they subside once and for all.*

*The new rhythm shifts into an easy, smooth pace. The rest of the world relaxes and trails in its wake.*

*All is remade. A changed world is waking. The storm has passed. The winds are quiet. The sky is softened. Running lines and flowing volumes appear. They trace a harmony and, like shifting light, make everything come alive.*

—— ✿ ——

As a signal, Joey's full hunger cry works, bringing his mother to him. Even before she has time to unbutton her blouse and get Joey to her breast, she has introduced four new elements into his world—sound, touch, motion, and a new position. These four, overlapping, make up the "envelope" that starts to push away the "vast empty spaces." Here is how these elements come into play.

First, Joey's mother enters his room calling his name. Like many mothers faced with a hungry, crying baby, she keeps on talking to him, sometimes nonstop, until the nipple is securely in his mouth. Exactly what she says is of little importance. "It's okay, Joey. It's okay. Mommy's hurrying as fast as she can. In just a minute now. It's okay, honey." She is talking to calm and reassure Joey (and also herself). What matters is the music and the sound, not the lyrics. She uses the music of her voice as a blanket to wrap Joey in to soothe him, or at least to hold the fort for a moment until he starts to feed. She also uses her voice as a pacemaker, at first going faster than the beat of Joey's cries, to override his rhythm; then she slows to bring him down with her to a less excited state. That is why the world appears to Joey to get slower. Her talking is, then, the first element to envelop him in gentleness. In fact, if Joey frets too much, he will remain too excited to suck at the breast. His mother is using some of her "instinctual" maternal knowledge to prepare him for the feeding—an exquisite regulation most mothers do without a thought.

Joey's mother now picks him up. She holds him first upright, while she gets ready for the feeding, and then horizontally to suckle, all the while patting and stroking him. This simple act changes Joey's world dramatically. To pick him up and hold him, his mother must touch him. Touch is the second new element in the "envelope." In the context of his sensation of exploding and expanding, this might feel like sudden containment, a boundary his world has bumped up against, but a boundary bringing some relief.

Repositioning is the third new element to alter Joey's world. A mother's first act (after talking) in this situation is to pick her baby up and hold him upright in a "hug position," his chest against her chest, his head on her shoulder, while she continues to prepare breast or bottle. Joey's mother does not know (except "intuitively") that this accomplishes two things at the same time. First, ventral-to-ventral contact (chest against chest)—the hug—is established. It seems to be the most powerfully calming type of human physical contact when someone is aroused and in distress. Joey will need or want to be hugged throughout his life, at any age, when his feelings are hurt, when he feels alone or insecure or sad. We will witness the power of the hug again when he is twelve months old (see chapter 7).

Second, the hug places Joey upright. This vertical position is very special for young infants. The feedback from Joey's muscles "tells" him about his position in space and has a strong influence on the state of his nervous system. Putting a baby into the upright position is, for his nervous system, like switching gears in a car. He becomes quieted physically, but more alert mentally in the sense of being more open to the sights and sounds around him. For instance, if the distress is not too great and the baby is only fretting, just repositioning him in an upright hug will calm him, and he will open his eyes wider and start to look around over his mother's shoulder. The combination of physical contact and upright position permits Joey to feel that "everything is shifting"— that is, reorienting or going back to normal. His world is "calmer."

Motion is the fourth element in the envelope now surrounding Joey's world. To reposition him, Joey's mother must move him in space. And she rocks him as she does so, along with her patting and stroking. Before his mother arrived in the room, Joey's subjective sense of motion was mainly of waves expanding explosively and collapsing back upon themselves. By moving him in space, his mother sets up competing motions. These weaken the force of his crying "motions."

Joey is beginning to learn that, when he is distressed, these changes caused by his mother's intervention signal a relief. He is beginning to form expectations of things to come. After all, he has had plenty of time to discover that when he is hungry his mother's appearance, and the way she treats him, will end up in a feeding. If we assume he suckles on the average five times a day, he has already had, at six weeks of age, two hundred and ten chances to learn this association. He is a smart baby. He is starting to become adept at such expectations. This growing expectation is the "faint promise" that "spurts." Hungry infants at the age of six weeks can be seen to quieten when mother arrives. I suspect this effect is partly due to the competing stimulation she creates. It is due also to the beginning of anticipation, which will become more evident around three months.

In spite of all these changes in Joey's world, the hunger remains. The talking and hugging and anticipation serve only to weaken the hunger enough to buy time. Joey feels this instability: "The pulsations of explosion and collapse are being tamed. But they are still there, still wild, still ready to break through."

Before the feeding starts, Joey must get the nipple into his mouth. This action is a well-choreographed *pas de deux*. On her side, the mother supports Joey's head and generally directs it toward where she is directing her breast, a fairly inexact spot. On his side, Joey does the fine-tuning. Like a compass needle caught in a magnetic field, his head swings in narrow arcs from side to side, guided by touch, until he has latched onto the nipple. These fine-tuning motions are built into Joey's reflexes; they are part of his genetic endowment.

Hunger propels Joey's search. He experiences his hunger internally, "at the very center of the storm." The nipple he is searching for (without knowing it, to be sure) is somewhere in this envelope, which now bounds his world. He would sense this process as, first, the "tug," the pulling together of two magnets. With their contact and then locking together, the nipple is securely in his mouth.

At this, the "point of contact" between his bodily sensation of hunger and his mouth, Joey begins to suck. Sucking is also an action pattern with which he is genetically endowed. All infants have roughly similar patterns of sucking: several bursts at a regular fast interval, then a pause, then another burst of regularly spaced sucks, then a pause, and so on. (The exact pattern is unique to each infant, as a fingerprint is.) It is this sucking that constitutes Joey's "new, fast rhythm."

Two things happen now. First, the act of sucking by itself, irrespective of the milk received, sets up the new rhythm in Joey's body. In fact, almost every muscle in his body recoordinates to most efficiently permit and sustain his sucking. As everything in him strains to strengthen that new rhythm, it begins to compete with and overtake the rhythm of the "slowly pulsing waves" of the pain of his storm. Second, Joey is swallowing. The warm liquid going down his throat must feel like a current flowing to the center of each of those waves. That current dissolves the chill of empty space, cools the fire of need, loosens the knot at the center of his hunger.

When a hungry baby of this age drinks, there appear to be two stages to the satisfaction of hunger. In the first stage of acute and powerful need, she drinks with total concentration. A relatively small amount of milk blunts that need, and the acute phase is over. (The milk releases biochemical signals in the stomach that feed back the information via the blood to the brain and there reduce the activity of the "hunger center.") In the next, less imperative, longer phase, a baby "shifts into an easy, smooth pace": she drinks the rest of the milk, but with less rapt attention and avidity. As she feels the rest of the world relaxing, so, too, do her own strung-up muscles relax. This second phase is contributed to, physiologically, by the volume of milk in the stomach, also acting as a signal to the brain.

With the shift to the second phase of hunger, Joey again becomes responsive to the world around him. With the acute phase past, he can drink and look and listen. Before, he could only drink. Parents intuitively understand this sequence. They can do pretty much anything during this first phase but break contact with breast or bottle. During the second phase, what they do depends on whether they want a fast, efficient feeding. If they do, they will avoid talking or making faces or doing all the other things whereby a parent can invite and engage a baby. The idea is not to distract and capture the baby's attention. On the other hand, the parent who wants to have a leisurely feeding can allow bouts of play to alternate with bouts of feeding. During this phase, a baby properly invited and stimulated to interact would rather play than eat. So a parent has to ration playfulness to get the meal finished.

It is not only that after the acute phase of hunger Joey opens up to the world again. In fact, he re-enters the world. Babies at this age have different states of consciousness, like sleep, drowsiness, alert inactivity, waking activity, crying, or acute hunger. These states are fairly distinct and separate. Babies pass from one state to the next in jumps, not gradually. Each state is like a step on a staircase, rather than a point on an incline. For this reason, there is a certain suddenness in a state change, more than for adults. Joey experiences the change in state from acute hunger as a sort of passage and arrival. "All is remade. A changed world is waking. The storm has passed. The wind is quiet. The sky is softened."

And in re-entering this "changed world," he most likely looks at his mother's face. It is there in his line of vision.

It is exactly the right distance away. The distance between the eyes of a baby at the breast and the mother's eyes is about ten inches, exactly the distance for the sharpest focus and clearest vision for a young infant. Finally, the features of a human face are ideally designed to match what infants are born to prefer to look at (as I shall discuss in greater detail in the next chapter).

So Joey, in the process of satisfying himself and being satisfied, gazes on the "running lines and flowing volumes" of his mother's face. Its forms are pleasing. There is now a correspondence (a "harmony") between his inner state of satisfaction-pleasure and the appearance of his mother's face. In fact, the inner pleasure will color his perception. Also, he is now open to notice the slight movements of her face and eyes that quicken him. And his new animation in response to her brings her face even more to life. This increase in animation combines with his new state of receptivity to act like "a shifting light," making "everything come alive." (Joey could, of course, at a different feeding or on another day, have shifted right into sleep, instead of alert inactivity.)

A vital association between the cycle of satisfaction-pleasure-reanimation and his mother's presence, face, and actions is being established for now and long into the future. We assume that the baby is starting to form a mental model, or representation, of his mother. This model will ultimately consist of many different pieces of interaction, of which this feeding sequence is one. Others would be the characteristic interaction of soothing him when he is distressed, or of stimulating him to evoke joy, and so on. We also assume that the mental model he builds of his mother will act as the prototype for what he will expect to happen with other loved persons whom he encounters in life.

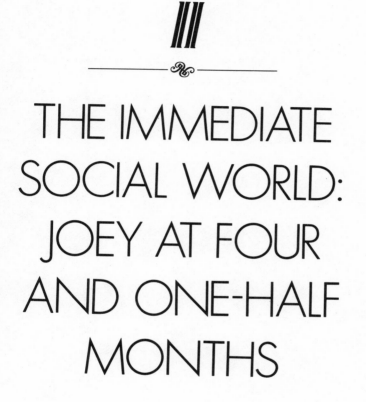

# THE IMMEDIATE
# SOCIAL WORLD:
# JOEY AT FOUR
# AND ONE-HALF
# MONTHS

*J*OEY has entered a short but extraordinary epoch in his life. Beginning between eight and twelve weeks, he undergoes a dramatic leap in development. Capacities for social interaction blossom: the social smile emerges, he begins to vocalize, and he makes long eye-to-eye contact. Almost overnight, he has become truly social. Still, his most intense social interactions are immediate, in that they are limited to the face-to-face and the "here and now, between us." In its undiluted form, this intense social world will last until he is about six months old. As a way of interacting with others and reading their behavior, it will last all his life.

It is a special social world for many reasons. First, there is the face itself. For Joey, the face is now the most attractive and fascinating object that exists. It obeys its own special rules and has evocative powers. This is true also for adults, though we are less intensely concentrated on faces. In your entire life, you have probably spent more time looking at faces than at any other class of object. You have been studying faces since you were born. You know what they are supposed to do, or not do, and when. You, and almost everyone, are a natural expert of facial expressions in all their subtleties. After all, it is mainly in the face that we feel we can read one another's feelings and intentions. And we start becoming experts at the very beginning of our lives.

The face makes a unique world for Joey. First, his visual system makes him find faces more pleasurable to look at than anything else. The long process of evolution has endowed Joey's vision with certain preferences. For instance, he prefers curves (like cheeks and eyebrows) to straight lines. He prefers strong light-dark contrasts (like the whites of the eyes against the pupil). He prefers acute angles (like the corners of the eyes) to obtuse angles. He is fascinated by symmetry in the vertical plane (like the mirror images of the left and the right sides of the face). He is now—compared with himself at six weeks—captivated by motion inside of a frame (like lips moving, in talk, within the borders of a face).

When you add up all these innate preferences, they almost spell out FACE. It is not that Joey actually has an innate preference for the face itself, but he does for so many of its essential features that it amounts to the same thing. To maximize the growth of human ties between baby and mother, the evolution of babies' visual preferences probably occurred simultaneously with that of the configuration of women's faces.

The face is special for two other reasons. First, a parent's face is not only alive; it is exquisitely responsive to what Joey does from moment to moment, so that Joey feels a special connection between himself and someone else. Second, after about two to three months of life, the human face has special powers. It acts like a trigger to set off social smiles and vocalizations from a baby. Since his seventh and eighth weeks of life, big smiles have been blossoming in response to his parents' actions. Joey has also started to babble back to them.

The other major event that ushers in this new social world is Joey's control of his gaze: where he looks, what he looks at, and for how long. By three and one-half months of age, he can control his gaze almost as well as an adult can. With this new ability in place, he can now start or stop a face-to-face interaction, because these interactions are built around mutual gaze. By simply looking at his mother, he can start an encounter, because she will almost always look back at him. He can then expand the encounter with an explosive smile, or end it by turning his head away and averting his eyes from her. He can refuse an invitation by declining to look, and terminate a social encounter by looking away definitively. He has become an expert in regulating such face-to-face social interactions.

Mutual gaze provides the structure for these interactions. Gazing back and forth, rather than talking back and forth, is the action. During this epoch, mutual gaze is the central event that everything else, like expressions of joy, turns or is built upon. And mutual gaze is an intense experience.

Babies act as if the eyes were indeed windows to the soul. After seven weeks of age, they treat the eyes as the geographic center of the face and the psychological center of the person. When you play peek-a-boo with a baby, she quickly shows some anticipatory pleasure as you lower the blanket to reveal your hair and forehead. But only when the baby sees your eyes does she explode in delight. Six-year-olds illustrate this psychological centrality of the eyes in a different way. When a six-year-old covers her eyes with her hands, and you ask her, "Can I see you?" she will answer, "No!" Although we used to think that the child could not imagine you could see her if she couldn't see you, that is not the problem. She knows perfectly well that you can see not only her but even her hands covering her eyes. What she really means by "No!" is, "If you can't see my eyes, you don't see *me.*" Seeing her means looking into her eyes.

The eyes are central for Joey and for us all. Looking at eyes that are looking back at you is something else again. First, you "feel" the mental life of the other person. Second, mutual gaze is extremely arousing. Adults will remain locked in silent mutual gaze—with no words spoken—for only seconds at a time unless they are falling in love, or are about to make love or to fight. Mutual gaze without speaking can be almost intolerable. In such animals as dogs, wolves, and great apes, mutual gaze provokes aggression. The submissive animal always looks away first, thus stopping the unfriendly approach of the other animal. Animal trainers in the circus use this knowledge to get an animal to approach (by giving it a challenging look in the eye) or to stop (by looking down and away). By carefully alternating the two, the trainer can get an animal to step into, and stop within, a series of rings.

In humans, mutual gaze seems to elicit either strong positive or negative feeling depending on the context. The staring games of children are based on this tendency, as are the staring maneuvers of adults. Who will look away first? And what has doing so lost or won?

The social interactions at this age, between Joey and his

mother or father, are not about anything. He and his caregiver have no specific subject matter, such as the weather or
an object, to discuss; no reason to give; no past to explain;
no future to plan. Their only "topic" is the single moment
happening now: two human beings mutually engaged.
These interactions' only goal is to sustain that experience.
They are not preliminary to something else: they *are* that
something. Also, with the exception of certain games like
peek-a-boo, these social interactions are largely spontane-
ous, neither Joey nor his mother knowing exactly the next
step. They invent it as they go along.

The possibility of such intense interactions is not limited to this age. It will continue throughout life, largely
in the background. But at certain moments it will surface
overwhelmingly: one day, when Joey is an adolescent, he
will look into a girl's eyes for minutes on end without
speaking, their only communication the play of facial expressions and shifts in breathing. Or, such moments will
blossom briefly when he shares some momentous experience with someone else.

There are several reasons Joey is immersed, even captured, in these special interactions during this epoch. Matu-
ration provided him with the behaviors and the urges to
carry on these encounters. Second, his innate preferences for
the human face, voice, and movements make his parents
both the natural trigger that releases his social behavior, and
the natural target toward which he directs that behavior.
Finally, what else can Joey do at this age? He is not only
exclusively interested in, he is limited to the social events
in the "here and now, between us." Even if he were interested in things outside the interpersonal, he couldn't do
anything about them. He can't yet move beyond these

boundaries. He can't reach, or give, or take, or point, or show, or ask, or comment upon anything. He is caught in this rich and intense world of the nonverbal, the purely interpersonal, the immediate. He is captured there by design and by default, at least until about five and one-half to six months of age.

This particular sequencing of developmental capacities may serve the purpose of permitting the baby to learn the crucial lessons of pure social interaction without the complications and diversions an object would create. Only once the purely social is established can an object be added. Along the same line of reasoning, why did nature not have babies learn language before about two years of life? Again, I would suggest that the baby has the all-important first task of learning the nonverbal basis of social interaction upon which language will later be built. And this primary task takes several years.

At that point, Joey will become both interested in the world of things and capable of dealing with that world. His hand-eye coordination and his hand-to-hand coordination will develop rapidly and permit him to reach and grasp and manipulate the world of inanimate objects. Then he will be able to turn to them and share them as a "topic" with his parents. But never totally. For the world of the "here and now, between us" is never lost to Joey. Another world has simply been added to it. But until that happens, during this brief epoch between two and six months Joey will live in this uniquely intense and immediate social world.

He is also coming to sense that he makes things happen in the world, that he is an agent. When he turns his head, the scene always changes. When he closes his eyes, the world always goes dark. When he moves his arm, he always feels the feedback from his muscles (the sensations from their movements) and their new position in space (the new muscular tensions due to gravity). In this way he is coming to appreciate that he is an actor, an active agent in events.

He is also coming to sense that he is a separate physical being from his mother, that he and she have different boundaries and are separate units that act and feel differently. When she moves, he does not feel any feedback from his muscles; when she speaks, he is not the author of her rhythm. When she touches him, he feels only touched. But when he touches himself, he feels at once that he is the toucher and the touched.

And he is beginning to sense that he has states of feeling, like happiness or hunger, that belong to him alone. When he is joyful, he feels a quickening, a rising arousal: he feels the muscles of his face and body pull into familiar configurations of tension and relaxation. He feels an inner sensation and an urge to act that go with that kind of quickening and those facial tensions. This familiar constellation of feelings happens not when his mother smiles, but only when he does.

Joey is starting to construct in his mind the world of people, including himself. He does this by first recognizing those happenings that are always the same: for example, when he wants to move his arm and does, he always feels the feedback from his muscles. Things that always go together and do not change are called *invariants*. Joey is now identifying those invariants that define the self and those that define other people.

When an infant can differentiate himself from his mother, and how this is accomplished, has been a heated question in most psychologies for a long time. The notion of an infant who searches for and identifies the invariant parts of experience helps provide an answer. Imagine three of the possible unchanging (invariant) elements of an arm movement. First, the volition to move the arm is the intention (usually beyond awareness) that precedes the movement and, so to speak, designs it in advance. Second, the muscular feedback comes during (and after) the execution of the planned movement. Third, the infant sees an arm move.

If Joey is acting alone in moving his arm, even in his mother's presence he will experience the volition, the feedback, and the sight of the motion. That constellation of invariants will begin to define a *self-event*. If Joey's mother moves her own arm in his presence, he sees an arm movement but experiences no volition and no feedback. Thus, that constellation of invariants begins to define other-person events as against self-events. Finally, if his mother moves Joey's arm for him (as when teaching him to clap his hands), he feels the feedback of his own arm's movements, and sees it move, but does not experience the volition that usually sets the movements going. This defines yet a third kind of event, the *self-with-another*.

This is how the infant begins to differentiate himself from his mother. It was once thought that this process was very slow, that babies live in some state of undifferentiated fusion with their mother for a long time—until the seventh or ninth month or so; and that in this state of merger, they do not know which behaviors or feelings belong to whom. We have recently come to recognize infants' ability early on to identify the invariants of their experience, and thus believe that discovering the distinction between self and other should be well under way by the third and fourth month of life.

Three major kinds of human event are now forming: events of the self; events of others; and events of the self-with-another. It is for this reason that I can now use *I, we,* and *her* when speaking in Joey's voice.

In short, Joey is starting to structure his social world. There are now distinct people in it: him and his mother and father at least, and all the familiar people intimately involved in his everyday life. Each of these caregivers has his or her own face and eyes and expressions and voice and gestures. And these people can act as agents to influence one another. They can also use their feelings, and the social behaviors that show feelings, in order to change the feelings of another person. With this much in place, Joey is capable of intricate face-to-face interaction.

Each of these new capacities, which permit the highly intricate social interactions of a four-and-one-half-month-old infant, is in itself a major developmental step. Their integration into coordinated social behavior is yet a higher step. If any of these capacities lags developmentally, the whole social interaction is likely to be slower to appear. If a major capacity is not there at all, the social interaction may suffer in proportion. Autistic infants, for instance, refuse to make and hold eye contact. They seem to find it distasteful rather than pleasant. Even if nothing else were amiss, this alone puts enormous limitations on a child's social experience and that of the parents. A caregiver who is unresponsive, depressed, or excessively preoccupied will also limit the range of social experiences.

Joey's developmental capacities at this age are, however, available and well integrated. And his parents are normally responsive most of the time. But, however available and sensitive, they will inevitably have periodic failures and make mistakes. These failures will be, if not too frequent, as important to his ultimate well-being as their successes. In the next two chapters, we discover the joys and hazards of Joey's new social world. In chapter 5, both he and his mother deal with an interaction that threatens to get out of hand; while in chapter 6, Joey's father helps him to cope with the diffuse stimulation of the world beyond the family.

# 5

## *A Face Duet:*
## *9:30 A.M.*

*J*OEY is sitting on his mother's lap, facing her. She looks at him intently but with no expression on her face, as if she were preoccupied and absorbed in thought elsewhere. At first, he glances at the different parts of her face but finally looks into her eyes.

He and she remain locked in a silent mutual gaze for a long moment. She finally breaks it by easing into a slight smile. Joey quickly leans forward and returns her smile. They smile together; or rather, they trade smiles back and forth several times.

Then Joey's mother moves into a gamelike sequence. She opens her face into an expression of exaggerated surprise, leans all the way forward, and touches her nose to his, smiling and making bubbling sounds all the while. Joey explodes with delight but closes his eyes when their noses touch. She then reels back, pauses to increase the suspense, and sweeps forward again to touch noses. Her face and voice are even more full of delight and "pretend" menace. This time Joey is both more tense and excited. His smile freezes. His expression moves back and forth between pleasure and fear.

Joey's mother seems not to have noticed the change in him. After another suspenseful pause, she makes a third nose-to-nose approach at an even higher level of hilarity, and lets out a rousing "oooOH!" Joey's face tightens. He closes his eyes and turns his head to the side. His mother realizes that she has gone too far, and stops her end of the interaction, too. At least for a moment, she does nothing. Then she whispers to him and breaks into a warm smile. He becomes re-engaged.

— ❧ —

*I enter the world of her face. Her face and its features are the sky, the clouds, and the water. Her vitality and spirit are the air and the light. It is usually a riot of light and air at play. But this time when I enter, the world is still and dull. Neither the curving lines of her face nor its rounded volumes are moving. Where is she? Where has she gone? I am scared. I feel that dullness creeping into me. I search around for a point of life to escape to.*

*I find it. All her life is concentrated into the softest and hardest points in the world—her eyes.*

*They draw me in, deep and deeper. They draw me into a distant world. Adrift in this world, I am rocked side to side by the passing thoughts that ripple the surface of her eyes. I stare down into their depths. And there I feel running strong the invisible currents of her excitement. They churn up from those depths and tug at me. I call after them. I want to see her face again, alive.*

*Gradually life flows back into her face. The sea and sky are transformed. The surface now shimmers with light. New spaces open out. Arcs rise and float. Volumes and planes begin their slower dance. Her face becomes a light breeze that reaches across to touch me. It caresses me. I quicken. My sails fill with her. The dance within me is set free.*

*Now we play chase-and-catch. She blows on the patch of water around me. It dances with her breezes. I glide upon it, picking up speed, exhilarated. Passing outside the boundary of her wind patch, I coast on my own through flat, still waters. Still moving, but more and more slowly without her breeze, I call after her. She responds and comes after me. She touches down a fresh breeze just in front of where I now am. Riding her wind, I gain speed. I call her to follow me again and to lead me forward. We pull each other forward in jumps. We play leapfrog with the dance between us.*

*Suddenly her wind shifts. The world of her face tilts up, new spaces open, and she approaches me with a fresh, strong breeze. It flies at me on its own rising song and envelops me. In its embrace I slip forward quickly in effortless delight. She moves back, and her wind eases off for a moment—but only long enough to gather new strength. The gust sweeps toward me again. I await its approach, excitement growing within me. The wind hits me. I heel sharply to the side, yet also leap ahead, borne gloriously on a crest of joy. This second gust passes, her wind dropping momentarily again. I am still moving at a thrilling speed, a little off balance. In the pause I try to right myself. But her next gust is rushing toward me, whipping up space and sound. It is upon me. It strikes. I try to meet its force, to run with it, but it jolts me through and through. I quake. My body stalls. I hesitate. Then I veer off. I turn my back to her wind. And I coast into quiet water, all alone.*

*This quiet place quells the turmoil inside me. It dies down and comes to a rest. I am comforted.*

*After a while in the stillness, a faint zephyr brushes the side of my head. It refreshes me. I turn and see it gently ripple the water under a softer sky.*

———— ✥ ————

As soon as Joey is placed on his mother's lap and looks at her, her face becomes the dominating presence in his world. It is such a potent stimulus for him that its actions will completely define his immediate world. He has entered a "face world."

At first, Joey's mother is fairly expressionless. Her mind is elsewhere, in a momentary reverie. She has not yet begun to interact with Joey even though she is looking at him. He looks quickly at her different features. He knows them thoroughly by now. He knows their characteristic movements. And he knows what is supposed to happen. Her remaining expressionless, even for a moment, when face to face and gazing at him is unusual, although it happens now and again. And it disturbs Joey that her face is "still and flat," its features motionless. This flatness must be eerie to Joey, who is immersed in her face as his immediate and entire world of stimulation. He feels that she—her vitality—is absent, and wonders where she went.

After about three months, when babies know what to expect in a face-to-face encounter with their mother, they get disturbed if she deviates far from the usual. And they are particularly perplexed if she suddenly stops interacting and her face becomes blank, or if they cannot rouse her to expression. In the well-known experiment called a *still-face procedure,* a mother, in the middle of an interaction, is asked to stop moving, to wipe all expression from her face, and just look at the baby. Infants after about two and one-half months of age react strongly to this still face. They look about. Their smiles die away, and they frown. They make repeated attempts to reignite the mother by smiling and gesturing and calling her. If they don't succeed, they finally turn away, looking slightly unhappy and confused.

Joey's mother has unwittingly performed a partial and short-lived "still face" for him by wandering into her own thoughts. This distresses Joey for several reasons. Where he has expected to enter the magic sound-and-light world of a face alive and responsive (the "riot of light and air at play"), he finds stillness and dullness. He not only reacts to the lack of expected stimulation, but may also identify with his mother; he may even imitate her and follow her into her state. Unable exactly to know her state, he can capture only the vague and confusing sense of her mentally hovering somewhere else. Somewhere he does not want to go. In identifying with her, he feels her emotional dullness creeping into himself.

The process of identification, whereby an infant—or anyone—feels like and acts like another person, and makes that person, in a sense, part of himself, is fascinating. Though little understood, it is of great clinical importance because many psychological problems can be seen as the result of a child's identifying with a parent who is frequently depressed, anxious, psychotic, or violent. Or, a child may be unable to identify, or be prevented (for whatever reason) from identifying, with positive aspects of one or the other parent and thus from making those aspects part of himself. This outcome is common in turbulent divorces where one parent strongly discourages any signs in the child of identification with the other parent.

Joey already has available two capacities essential for identification. First, he imitates, almost automatically, the facial expressions and gestures of others. In fact, he has been performing parts and pieces of these imitations almost since birth. Second, he, like an adult, is susceptible to emotional contagion. Thus, when someone yawns, you are likely to yawn. When she smiles (even when you don't know what about), you may feel happier and begin to smile yourself. When she cries, your eyes may moisten. Newborn babies cry when they hear the cry of other babies in the neighboring cribs in the nursery. This contagion goes beyond mere imitation. The other person's emotional state invades you, so to speak, to set up a responsive feeling within you.

Imitation and contagion may permit Joey to identify early with his mother's state of distracted preoccupation. Though momentarily preoccupied, she soon responds to him. Imagine, however, a mother who is chronically preoccupied (as by trouble with her husband or her career) so as to be only partially "there" when with him face to face. Or, a mother (or another caregiver) who is depressed and rarely available even when present. The child of either sort of mother has to learn to have different expectations. He learns to construct a mental picture of a mother who is there as a physical presence but is, as an animated responsive force, present only intermittently or weakly. The child who wanted to achieve and maintain a high level of arousal and joy, would have to avoid direct contact with her, even in her presence. He would learn to look elsewhere for the needed stimulation. Or, he would learn to make extraordinary efforts to charm his mother, to pull her along—to act as an antidepressant to her, who should be responding so to him. Joey has, however, other expectations of his mother. To be aroused, he does not have first to turn himself on. He can turn to her, not away from her, to seek out the strong spark of her animation.

He finds it in her eyes. In fact, he is pulled to her eyes because of the vivid and stimulating qualities I have spoken of: the contrast of light and dark, their curves, angles, brilliance, depth, and symmetry. In the past two months, since his seventh week, his mother's eyes have come to dominate the other features of her face. They are the most fascinating target of Joey's vision. Locked into mutual gaze with her, he passes into the "distant world" of her eyes alone.

Mutual gaze is, indeed, a world within a world. Looking into eyes that are looking back into yours is like no other experience with another person. You seem to feel and follow vaguely the mental life of the other. When in a mutual gaze, you (or Joey) periodically shift your gaze back and forth from the other's left eye to the right. And that person does the same with you. (Someone who doesn't do it is not all there for you.) Each of these rapid shifts, in slightly altering the perspective of each of the gazers, also alters—sometimes dramatically, sometimes ever so slightly—what each sees. These shifts in both direction and focus seem to each gazer like a reflection of the other person's thinking. "I am rocked side to side by the passing thoughts that ripple the surface of her eyes."

"The invisible currents of her excitement," which Joey feels running strong, reflect the arousal so powerfully evoked by mutual gaze. Arousal is an internal tension that mounts, a rise in animation or excitation, a growing readiness to act, either lovingly or hostilely. If nothing gets in the way of this silent mutual looking, the internal tension mounts rapidly. Usually we modulate this tension by doing things that distract us from it, like talking or gesturing or "drifting away." You can sense the rises and falls in another's level of arousal through many subtle cues: changes in breathing, shifts in the sharpness of visual focus, slight movements about eyes or mouth. Babies are alert to the same cues.

It is during this experience of Joey's own and his mother's rising and falling arousal that he feels the "invisible currents": They "tug at me. I call after them." In this deep sounding of his mother, Joey is summoning her back to "life."

And she responds. She returns her full attention to him and eases into a smile. As she lets the currents of life within her flow back, Joey experiences her face as sea and sky "transformed." Specifically, he watches the movements of each facial feature as the smile breaks over her face. After all, each feature for Joey is still also a form in space with its own architecture and luminosity and movement. As the choreography of her smile proceeds, the skin's tautness changes, and smile wrinkles appear: "The surface now shimmers with light." Her cheeks widen, and her mouth opens: "New spaces open out." The curve of her cheek is raised, and the corners of her lips pull up: "Arcs rise and float." As the architecture of her face shifts, "volumes and planes begin their slower dance."

Joey also experiences the entire transformation as a demonstration of the return of her life force, a return that affects him directly and immediately. "Her face becomes a light breeze that reaches across to touch me. It caresses me."

In reaching across to touch him, her smile exerts its natural evocative powers and sets in motion its contagiousness. Her smile triggers a smile in him and breathes a vitality into him. It makes him resonate with the animation she feels and shows. His joy rises. Her smile pulls it out of him. Then Joey himself fully releases it from inside: "I quicken. My sails fill with her. The dance within me is set free." He is both responding and identifying now.

Once a pair of smiles has passed between a mother and a baby of this age, a process has already been set in motion. What happens is this. Joey's smile and his mother's are slightly out of phase with each other. That is as it should be, since a smile takes time to grow on the face, to reach its peak, and to fade. When his mother's smile is close to its peak, it triggers Joey's smile. And when Joey's smile hits its peak, it reanimates her fading smile. By remaining out of phase, they keep restarting the other and prolong the duet. It is this passing in and out of her field of animation that makes Joey feel as if he were moving into and then beyond the local breezes she creates with her sequence of smiles. This is the "game of chase-and-catch" they play. Each person's smile being both cause and result of the other's smile, they end up pulling each other "forward in jumps": "We play leapfrog with the dance between us."

Such an alternating pattern between mother and baby becomes common after three months. It occurs in vocalizing back and forth as well as in smiling back and forth. It is the baby's first and principal lesson in turn taking, the cardinal rule for all later discourse between two people. Thus, this simple playful exchange lays down one of the foundations of social interaction.

Furthermore, Joey can now think in terms of himself taking an initiative in order to accomplish a goal. He has a sense both of himself as the author of his own actions, and of his actions as having predictable consequences. He feels himself to be an agent in a causal chain of events. "*I* call after her," he says. "She responds and comes after me."

This new sense of himself as actor and agent has come about during the last month or so because he has repeatedly experienced events like sucking his thumb or vocalizing and gotten in response a smile or words. For instance, in thumb sucking, he senses his volition to suck his fingers (the wish); he senses the execution of that wish in his arm movement (the action); he senses the feedback, his own arm's new position in space telling him that the event has occurred as planned (the execution); and he senses the desired result of getting his fingers in his mouth (the goal). All these, occurring together, form a single constellation of events (they are the invariants I spoke of before).

He has also come to realize that his mother is a different and separate actor-agent. Usually, it is clear to Joey who is the agent of a particular action, and who its object. For instance, when his mother just smiled spontaneously, coming out of her reverie, she was clearly the agent and he the object. Later on, he will initiate a smile to start things again where he is clearly the sole agent. However, during this particular moment filled with linked smiles, back and forth, Joey will probably feel that the smiles are jointly initiated. His mother has willed and executed her own smiles, but he has called them forth. Similarly, he has willed and executed his own smiles, but she has evoked them. There are many such moments of joint initiation and mutual creation. They are the stuff of being-with-another-person that constitute the ties of attachment. So much of attachment consists of the memories and mental models of what happens between you and that other person: How you feel with them. What they can make you experience that others cannot. What you can permit yourself to do or feel or think or wish or dare—but only in their presence. What you can accomplish with their support. What parts, or view, of yourself need their eyes and ears as nourishment.

"Suddenly her wind shifts." It is at this moment that Joey's mother alters: instead of just returning his smile, she goes into higher gear. She breaks the easy pattern of exchanging smiles and makes a strong bid for a more intense engagement by putting on an exaggerated expression of mock surprise. Mothers commonly make that face for exactly this purpose, and it is ideally suited to activate a baby. The mother usually displays the mock surprise with much gusto. She throws her head up and back ("the world of her face tilts up"); then she raises her eyebrows, widens her eyes, and opens her mouth ("new spaces open"). At the same time she approaches Joey's face with her own in its new expression. These coordinated movements seem to Joey like "a fresh, strong breeze": "It flies at me." At the same time her bubbling sounds crescendo with the mock-surprise expression and make up the "rising song" of the breeze that envelops Joey.

The effect of this action by a mother is usually dramatic. It activates the baby. The more stimulation a baby is exposed to, the more he will be activated or excited. This direct relationship between the intensity of stimulation from the outside (performed by the mother) and that of the excitation evoked in the baby is a general rule for mother-infant interactions. In this case, Joey's mother has raised her level of stimulation from well-modulated smiles to the mock surprise plus vocalization, plus physical approach. Not only does Joey experience an immediate jump in excitation, but he doesn't have to do anything except let his mother's accelerated animation play upon his responsive nervous system: "I slip forward quickly in effortless delight."

His mother's expression of mock surprise is, in fact, the prelude to initiating a special game, the nose-touching game. With dramatic sweeps forward, face alight, voice in play, she touches her nose against his and then retreats, with a suspenseful pause to prepare for the next advance. She makes three such sweeps forward, each one a little more dramatic and stimulating. There are a host of such international baby games—"I'm gonna get ya," "tickle-the-tummy," "round and round the garden," and so on; and they follow an intricate and interesting pattern. While the idea is simply to have fun, it is achieved by conforming to certain rules.

Thus, the moves in the game have to be stimulating enough to keep the baby animated. But they can't be too stimulating lest the baby become too excited and disorganized right away. On the other hand, they can't be too dull or the baby will get bored. They must stay in an optimal range of stimulation to keep the baby in an optimal range of excitement and pleasure. Maintaining this range is not easy. Babies quickly become familiarized with anything that is repeated. It becomes habitual, and they become bored. For this reason, the mother cannot make the exact same moves over and over in a repetitive game, but must vary them with each successive move. So she intuitively turns the game into a theme and variation, where each repeat is different enough from the previous one to prevent the baby's habituation and to hold his interest.

Joey's mother does these things without thinking, as part of "intuitive" parental behavior. It is astounding how many things an average parent knows to do intuitively. For instance, most parents change the way they speak when talking to a baby. They raise the pitch of their voice. They slow the rhythm. They make the melody more pronounced, more singsong. And they soften some of the sounds: "pretty rabbit" becomes "pwitty wabbit." They do this unaware and without having been taught. Even four- to five-year-old children who have no younger brothers and sisters do it when faced with a baby. These behaviors are not only intuitive but also biologically appropriate. Babies naturally prefer sounds spoken at a higher pitch, not too fast, and with melody and softened consonants. Evolution has apparently shaped parental behavior to complement babies' auditory preferences.

The use of a theme-and-variation format to regulate a baby's level of arousal is also intuitive parental behavior. And that is exactly what Joey's mother is trying to do by acting more animated in each successive repeat, or variation.

Some babies, and Joey is one of them, seem to love to play near their upper level of tolerance for excitation. It is like flirting with danger. During this nose-to-nose game, each lunge forward by his mother, with her face and voice in full play, feels to Joey like an exhilarating gust of wind. If he can stay upright and ride with it, the lift and speed are thrilling. And so it is the first time she approaches, and also the second, but less so. The third time, the force of her approach is too strong, and Joey is still "off balance" from the second gust: that is, his level of excitation is not yet under his control again. So when the third approach "strikes," Joey can no longer handle the stimulation. It "jolts him through and through," and he starts to fight it. Having passed beyond his optimal zone of excitation, he falters on the brink of becoming overwhelmed, fearful, and disorganized.

Faced with overstimulation, Joey has some simple options for dealing with this potential disaster. The simplest is to turn his head and eyes away from his mother. And that is what he does: "I veer off. I turn my back to her wind." This action accomplishes three goals. First, since the source of stimulation is no longer in view, it is no longer directly acting upon him. Second, he can choose what he wishes to look at, and will pick something much less stimulating so that his excitation, including his heart rate, can subside into an acceptable range: "I coast into quiet water, all alone." And there he can recover a range where he is again open and susceptible to external stimulation. Finally he is sending his mother a signal, telling her what to do next. And she will pick it up. Parents and caregivers need this kind of constant feedback to know what to do, and when. Being a "good" parent is in large part knowing how to readjust behavior.

Joey's mother did indeed overstimulate him, and not for the first or the last time in his life. In any lively parent-baby interaction, this is bound to happen as each one pushes at the limits. You can't expand the limits without pushing at them. And when you push at them, you inevitably make mistakes. These necessary mistakes are potentially of great value, helping infants to develop their own ways of coping with a variety of experiences and people. Joey has also just dealt successfully with overstimulation and overexcitation all by himself—no small lesson. And finally, his mother's miscalculation in exceeding his upper level of tolerance does not constitute a trauma or a tragedy. Joey has taken care of the situation rather well—so well that, after a moment or two, he is again ready to be invited back into an interaction. But the invitation will work only if it is very gentle—that is, at a low level of stimulation. His mother has intuitively understood what happened. She pauses for an appropriate time and invites him back with a whisper and a gentle smile. Since Joey is ready, her invitation feels like a "faint zephyr" brushing his head, and her smile like a "gentle ripple." He is back in the social interaction, "face to face, here and now, between us." And soon, because they both know how to signal to the other and to make the needed adjustments, they will retrieve their rapport and start another game of improvisation.

# 6

## Time, Space, and Flow: Noon

*L*ATER that morning, a Sunday, Joey's father takes him next door to a brunch at the house of family friends. His mother will come later. His father carries him on his hip. There are already several people there. Joey's father walks around saying hello, still carrying Joey. People move about and take seats, holding their coffee and food. His father then sits in a deep chair with Joey on his lap facing out looking at the room of people. An easy conversation picks up. Sometimes Joey seems attentive to the flow of conversation in a vague way. Sometimes he looks at the window in the far wall facing him. Sometimes his attention just wanders. One of the guests says something funny. People laugh. Then one woman on the other side of the room lets out a more explosive, louder laugh. Joey quickly turns to look at her. But he soon relaxes back against his father.

*I ride the air with Daddy. . . .*

*We enter a place where people and things move every
which way. Each planet or moon or comet is on its own
course, headed to an unknown place. And each moves at its
own speed and in its own time. . . .*

*We stop and settle. . . .*

*The music moves around us, going from person to person. Daddy takes up the music. It vibrates against my back.
He lets it go, and it floats away somewhere else. . . .*

*I am rising and falling on the easy tide of his breathing.
. . .*

*Over there is a frame. In it, an intense warm glow. When
people pass it, the intensity in the frame empties, then
quickly fills up. In my room at home, my morning-intense-
warm glow dances more slowly. . . .*

*The music reappears and swells. It rushes across the room
and crashes on the face of a woman. My head jerks toward
her. . . .*

*Daddy hugs me closer to him, and I feel better.*

— ❧ —

As adults, we take for granted that when we move forward
in space, we create an apparent visual flow of all the objects
around us. When, for instance, you enter a room and walk
toward someone at the far end (as Joey's father does), all the
people and tables and lamps between you and that person,
on the left side, appear to flow toward you and pass you
on the left; and all the things to the right of that person
appear to flow visually toward you and pass you on the
right. Thus, visually speaking, by walking forward you
create two broad rivers of space that divide at your destina-
tion and flow around you on each side. The person you are

headed for does not enter the visual flow. He is the still point, like the vanishing point of perspective in a painting done from a traditional spatial point of view. Your movement creates a coherent organization of the space around you.

When Joey's father, on entering the room, walks over to say hello to someone, he naturally experiences this visual flow of space created by his movement. But Joey, though carried by him, does not, even though he is moving through space just as much as his father is. The reason Joey does not experience these two rivers of visual flow is that he has never moved through space by himself. Joey won't start to crawl for another three to five months, and he won't walk for another six to nine months or so. So far, all the movements that have displaced him in space have been caused by someone else. It seems that the human visual system relies on the experience of self-propelled motion to develop fully the capacity to see space in terms of a visual flow while moving. It is a learned capacity based on active motor experience.

So, instead of a spatial world organized by a directional visual flow, Joey is in a relatively chaotic world. Here he perceives people and objects as planets, moons, or comets moving "every which way," each "on its own course, . . . at its own speed, . . . in its own time." For Joey, the spatial flux remains unorganized. He is not bothered by this lack of organization or coherence: it does not violate anything he knows. It is just the way the world is for now.

Most infants, roughly until they can crawl or walk, seem readily to accept being moved through space in, to us, the most unlikely ways. At one moment, a baby is lying on her back, face up, going backward in a carriage with the hood cutting off half the visual field—but, at the next corner, when the carriage is turned around, she is suddenly going forward. And then a minute later, when the sun is hidden by clouds and it is not so bright, the hood of the carriage is taken down and a much larger slice of the visual field is rushing by. Infants tolerate these changes because they do not so far violate any privileged visual or vestibular conventions for moving through space.

Joey knows perfectly well, however, that he is moving. Although his passive motion does not organize the space, his well-functioning vestibular system tells him when he is moving and when he and his father stop. Once they have settled in the chair, Joey has a new point of reference—immobility—with which he is thoroughly familiar.

As for Joey's temporal world, there is clock time and there is subjective time. Clock time moves only and always forward, at an even rate. It never stops. Subjective time, on the other hand, can double backward and replay events in memory. It moves at variable speeds, sometimes faster, sometimes slower. And there are often gaps in subjective time as if the clock stopped when we weren't noticing and then started up again. Do infants experience subjective time as adults do? The biggest problem with this question is that it is not clear how adults experience the flow of subjective time. For instance, as I was writing this paragraph this morning, the phone rang. I ran quickly to get it so it would not wake my wife. I still had my uncapped pen in my hand as I stood in the hall holding the phone. It was my friend Tom calling to say that he couldn't pick me up as planned, but would meet me at the train station to go to the city in forty-five minutes. While he was telling me that, I had a visual image of him coming down the station ramp to an exact place on the platform where I would be standing, and was slightly annoyed that he would be late for that, too. After a gap when I do not recall what he or I said, I worried that my voice would wake my wife. When I thought that, I pictured her in bed as if I were standing or hovering in the air in the bedroom. Then there was another gap, after which I remember only looking at a pattern on the floor. I recall nothing further until I was back in my study packing my things in my briefcase. I do not remember ending the phone call or returning to my study, but obviously I did both.

This recollection of a recent experience illustrates what subjective time may feel like when you are performing fairly routine tasks with neither important events nor strong emotions to organize your attention tightly. There are several striking things about this vignette. First, subjective time is discontinuous: the flow is filled with gaps when my consciousness of the flow stops and suddenly reappears farther downstream in "real" clock time. Second, you can be in two time frames at once: as I am talking on the phone with my pen in my hand, now; and at the station "seeing" my friend come down the platform, an hour or so into the future. Third, you can be in two or three different places at the same time: as I am in the hall on the phone, at the station, in the bedroom watching my wife sleep (each place "lived" with a different and fluctuating amount of attention). And finally, you can take pieces of discontinuous action and disparate time frames and places and weave them all together into a reasonably coherent story of something that happened at a particular time, as on this morning. A story held together with a theme, subplots, and all the devices for creating meaning that make our daily lives appear to be coherent and understandable. For instance, I fill in all the gaps with my knowledge of how the world generally works so that I don't have to remember exactly what really happened.

I could, as an example, structure this incident around the theme of "How difficult my friend Tom is." He calls early in the morning, interrupts my work, makes me run for the phone so it doesn't wake up the whole family, changes our plans at the last minute, and he will be late in the new plan anyway. Told that way, the vignette seems to have a clear story line. We act as if most of our lives were lived that way, when in fact our brains function in such a way that many different and possibly unrelated things are going on in parallel. We choose from these many mental events those that will permit us to weave a coherent story of our lived experience.

But Joey so far experiences events as loosely or not at all connected in time. Thus, in Joey's text, each distinct focus of attention or delimited experience is followed by ellipses indicating a probable gap in his experience. Joey is not yet old enough to be able or to need to rework the sequence of his experiences into a coherent whole. Where adults feel fragmented and disorganized when they cannot render their mental activities into a reasonably comprehensible and coherent whole, infants of Joey's age accept their experience as they live it in the present moment. Here Joey has had at least eight discontinuous and loosely related experiences: being carried by his father; moving through the room; stopping and sitting; the flow of conversation; riding the tide of his father's breathing; looking at the window and recalling the morning sunpatch in his bedroom; the woman's laughter; and his father's physical reassurance.

Each of these experiences exists separately in its own subjective time frame.

How might Joey experience memories of the past? Recalled memories create a parallel time frame—*then* and *now*. At four and a half months, Joey is just old enough to consider two different things at the same time. Why can he not also experience a past event along with a present one? Looking across the room, Joey sees the window there as an "intense glow." When someone passing in front of the window blocks its light, he experiences the intensity as "emptying"; and, as they pass by, it "fills up" with intensity again. This window, a square of bright light especially dazzling in the darker room, reminds Joey of the morning sunpatch on his bedroom wall. The memory of the sunpatch occurs as an "image" in Joey's mind, and he then compares it with the directly perceived image of the window. But Joey does not know that one of these images is a memory. He has simply two different forms of experience.

Joey is not hallucinating. He has not lost contact with reality. He does not get confused between remembered and perceived images. Rather, he is experiencing two different kinds of mental event at the same time. Because the remembered image is also being experienced here and now, it is not subjectively a memory. It is just as much alive for him but with a different kind of life. Joey simply has a wider tolerance for what belongs in the present than adults generally do. Thus, everything is in time present for Joey. And instead of the coherent time line usually assumed by adults, Joey's is a present filled with vivid diversity. He cannot yet reframe his eight experiences into the comprehensive time frame of a story as he will be able to do when he is four years old (see part V).

Time and space have their own laws that all bodies, human or not, must obey. But Joey at this age, as I have mentioned, is particularly sensitive to and captivated by humans and what they do. For instance, he becomes aware of the spatial flow of conversation, because the human voice means a lot to him. He does not follow the spatial pattern of sounds made by spoons against saucers, or by doors closing and chairs being scraped over the floor, which are also going on in the same room—and may be to an autistic child more compelling than the human voices.

Joey, of course, follows the general sounds and not the specific words of conversations. It is as though he were following the melody around an orchestra, from the strings to the woodwinds to the brass and back: "The music moves around us, going from person to person. . . . It floats away." Because Joey is hearing the music and not the lyrics, he has a sensibility different from the adults' about what is harmonious. The woman's laugh strikes Joey as a major violation in the music. What he does not know, and the adults do, is that someone has just said something funny to which her laughter is an understandable response. On the other hand, what the adults fail to register consciously, but Joey perceives, is that her laughter is forced and too loud: there is, in the music, a discordant note. Discordant enough to startle and upset Joey, as though a shot had been fired: "My head jerks toward her." The effect on Joey is so strong that his father senses, probably without being aware of it, that his baby needs to be reassured. He pulls Joey closer, and the restabilization given by greater physical contact helps him to "feel better" and continue to follow the music.

In this situation, the adults have taken an event, the woman's laughter, and placed it in a total social context, within a story. Supported by this context, her laughter is appropriate, and the way she laughed a minor detail. Only Joey, who remains in the unmitigated present moment, sees her raucous laughter as a cardinal event.

Physical contact with his father, his mother, or another caregiver must define a different kind of space for Joey from the space "over there." It is a privileged space which obeys the laws of emotional relatedness. What is being regulated in this close space is not distance, directionality, or position but security, comfort, and intimacy.

Similarly, an infant may also experience time differently when engaged in a face-to-face encounter with a parent. As in the "face duet" earlier this same morning, the infant's attention is so captured by the active engagement with the parent that, so long as that attention remains unbroken, there is only one long present moment. The structure of Joey's subjective time is different here. In this moment, there is no active engagement between Joey and his father, at least not of the kind that holds Joey's entire attention. He is left free to have his attention wander here and there. And thereby he experiences time as more fractured and less coherent. In contrast, in the "face duet," the encounter itself tightly organized Joey's mental activities; thus, the interactive event imposed cohesion on a long stretch of his experience. In a sense, parents can, by providing captivating interaction, help the child to begin to organize his own diverse experiences into a meaningful sequence.

# THE WORLD OF MINDSCAPES: JOEY AT TWELVE MONTHS

$\mathcal{J}$OEY is in the process of making two great discoveries that go hand in hand. First, that he has his own private mindscapes: that is, mental landscapes that are not visible to others unless he makes an attempt to reveal them. And, second, that it is possible to share a mindscape of his own with someone else. The two discoveries are developmental leaps. Once he becomes capable of taking them, they will determine his view of the human world for the rest of his life.

A *mindscape* contains intentions, desires, feelings, attention, thoughts, memories, all those vivid events that occur in an individual's mind but are invisible to others. They make up the subjective landscapes of one's private world. This interior world can, however, be revealed and made visible to others—never exactly, but enough so that two people believe they have the same thing in mind. When that happens, they are sharing an *intersubjective mindscape*. Furthermore, one person's mindscape can be almost completely occupied with what is going on in another person's mind. An exaggerated example of such intersubjectivity is when someone can say to another, "I know that you know that I know . . . ," or, "I feel that you feel that I feel. . . ." However intricate this may sound, it is the routine stuff of being intimate with another person.

Once a baby starts to become a reader of the human heart and mind, the central social action is now and forever the human drama made up of motives and feelings and desires and goals, the invisible subjective contents of mind.

How can we know that Joey has made the major developmental leap of discovering mindscapes toward the end of the first year? The clues are simple. For instance, if Joey is looking at a toy across the room and is interested in it, he may turn to look at his mother to enlist her attention and help. If at that moment she is not looking at the toy and he wants her to look at it, beginning at around nine months he will point at the toy with his arm outstretched and his index finger cocked. But he does not simply point. He looks down the barrel of his pointing arm at the toy and then shifts his gaze back to mother's face, then back to the object—and so back and forth, until she turns her head to look at the toy.

The important "action" for Joey in this example is gaining his mother's attention. Attention is a subjective state of mind, a mindscape. It is also accompanied by overt behavior, head turning and gaze direction, that reflects pretty clearly part of what is going on inside the mind. The point is that Joey has begun to shift his central concern away from the overt behavior between himself and others—events that are out in the open and can be sensed directly, such as physical gestures, facial expressions, voices. He is now becoming concerned more with the mental state, the mind-scape, behind such overt behavior.

In this connection, Joey has recently become interested in hidden objects as well as in hidden mental events. Until now he would not look for an object after it was hidden from view. He acted as if it had stopped existing when he could no longer see it. Now he searches for it when it is hidden. It is out of sight but not out of mind. Things can now exist in the mind alone. The reason is partly that he now has a more developed memory. He can recall things or events that are not present at the moment. He can evoke them from his store of memories and have them come alive on his mental stage as an image, a mindscape. At this epoch, he also becomes fascinated by games of hiding: here, too, one must remember or imagine what one cannot see. The universal favorite is peek-a-boo in all its variations.

Intentions are also becoming part of his subjective land-scape. In the past few months, Joey has begun to act as if he knows that he has intentions in his mind, and that there is more than one way to reveal them. He also knows that another person can have the same or complementary inten-tion. If his mother has a cookie in her hand and Joey wants it, he knows how to reveal his intention. He stretches out his arm, his open hand directed toward the cookie. He looks back and forth between the cookie, his hand opening and closing, and his mother's face, and vocalizes. And if that doesn't work, he will find another way to reveal the content of his mind until his mother "gets it" and changes her intention along the lines he has in mind. He may pull on her skirt, with a rising, insistent vocal intonation, still look-ing at the cookie. What he wants is clear. He wants her to read his mind (she is being quite unresponsive here). And, if necessary, he is willing to try several other means of revealing his mindscape. The point is that only if he gets her to attend to him and his mindscape can she respond appropriately.

A mindscape can also be about feelings. When Joey sees something strange and novel for the first time (for instance, a clown who starts to cry), he may feel a mixture of fear and attraction. In fact, for an instant he seems not to know which way to feel. Beginning around nine to twelve months, he will then look to his mother's face to see which way she has taken it. Is it to be feared? Or, to be approached with joyful curiosity? If his mother shows a happy, relaxed face, Joey will approach the new thing with a smile. If an apprehensive face, Joey will shy away and even get upset. He is now evaluating his mother's mental state of feeling in order to regulate his own feeling state. In the same way, a baby who has fallen down, and is surprised but not quite hurt, will first read her mother's face to see whether to cry or smile.

Joey has discovered what philosophers call the *theory of separate minds:* that he and his parents have different mindscapes but can also share the same mindscape. His discovery of intersubjectivity constitutes an enormous change in his development. Beginning now, and probably for the rest of his life, he will interpret human actions, at least in part, in terms of the mental states behind the actions. He will focus on the fit between the mindscapes of others and his own. Let's suppose a baby girl around this age comes upon a new toy truck and gets enthusiastic about it. She will look to her mother to see whether her mother shares her own high enthusiasm for this terrific new toy. Suppose the mother, for whatever reasons at this point in social history, wants her to play with "girl toys," but not "boy toys." The little girl will start to learn that her mother shares her enthusiasm only in respect to certain kinds of toy. When it comes to trucks and such, her mother, being a modern woman, would never say "No!" or anything so blatantly disapproving. The effect is more subtle than that. The girl will simply feel that her inner mental state of enthusiasm is not particularly desirable if the mother responds with faint enthusiasm, or even undesirable if the mother responds with a rebuke or not at all. The sharing or nonsharing of mental states is a powerful way to shape another person's behavior. The same kind of process goes on in any relationship. Husbands and wives are constantly negotiating or openly fighting about which mental states are sharable and which must remain the private property of only one of the pair.

The possibility of fitting mental states between people raises the possibility of misreadings and failure to fit. For example, two-year-old babies are remarkably curious and exploratory. When in a parent's lap, one may vigorously explore with a finger the parent's mouth or nose or even eyes. The parent who experiences this exploration as a physical violation or an act of aggression, may not only react with anger but also attribute hostility to the baby. The parent is likely to follow this feeling up with a rebuke, a slap, or some rejection of the baby, who had only been doing what comes naturally at that age. As a result, there is now, between parent or caregiver and baby, a gross misunderstanding about motives.

Often the baby becomes both confused by the parent's lack of correspondence with her, the baby's, mental state and also upset or hurt or frightened because of being rebuked or rejected. The baby is likely at this point to repeat the exploration—to clarify the confusion, or to evoke a different response this time, and also to get back at the parent for his or her response. Because there is now a note of true assertiveness in the baby's action (it is still not necessarily the main motive), the parent assumes that his or her original (mis)understanding of the situation has been confirmed: that the baby had, indeed, been acting aggressively.

If this situation is repeated, the parent's false interpretation may become the infant's and later the child's official and accepted one. The infant's acts of exploration, directed at her parents, may well take on an aggression that was not originally hers. The baby, too, may come to see herself as aggressive, even hostile. Someone else's reality has become hers. Thus, the failure of intersubjectivity can introduce a lifelong distortion.

At this same time, Joey is making sharper distinctions between people. People look and sound different; more important, they make him feel emotionally different. There is the world of strangers who make him wary. There is another world of familiar people. And there is more and more the special world of his primary care-giver—in Joey's case, his mother. You might think that his mother would be most important and special to him at birth or right after, and perhaps she is from the point of view of fulfilling his physical needs. In Joey's mind, in the past months, she is becoming even more important emotionally. He now has a sense of *his* need for her presence. His attachment to her is becoming more evident to him; it is not necessarily stronger. This relative shift of his need for her from physical gratification (as in feeding) to emotional regulation (as in feeling secure) is evident in Joey's attachment to his mother. He now cries when she leaves the room. He tries to call her back. He is miserable, sometimes for brief periods and sometimes for long ones, during her absence. Even when she is not present, she remains a permanent part of his subjective landscape. And when she is there, he is now deeply attentive to her emotional availability to him—that is, to her subjective state. Joey's attachment to his mother has not really changed. It has been there from birth and will continue to develop. Only now he can actually experience this attachment and can act on it with newly developed behaviors and strategies. And, of course, if his mother worked regularly, he would develop the same attachment not only to her but also to his daytime caregiver.

Finally, Joey has been walking for the past month. This wonderful new ability also helps consolidate these changes in his world view. It gives him a larger sweep of space in which to experience his intentions and desires and goals and feelings. Moving through space—as he has been doing since he was crawling—accomplishes something else as well: it permits Joey to see the same thing from different points of view. For instance, he can see a chair from the front. If he then walks to the right and forward, he sees it from the side, or from the bottom while crawling, and then from the top as he pulls up to stand. A physical change in perspective is essential to imagining another's state of mind, compared with your own. Being able to shift his geographical viewpoint by moving will help Joey shift his psychological viewpoint by empathic imagining.

At twelve months, Joey has stepped into a new world where the center of gravity has shifted from overt physical events in the here and now to hidden subjective events spread over past, present, and immediate future. In the next two chapters, he experiences the world of mindscapes and elaborated attachment in two different events on the same morning: a visit to a train station; then back home where he finds a toy he has momentarily lost.

# 7

*A Voyage:*
## 10:30 A.M.

*J*OEY has gone with his mother to a large waiting
room in a train station. After a while he wanders away from
her, meets a little girl, gets lost, becomes frightened, and
then finds his mother again. She takes him in her arms and
calms him.

— ❧ —

*We are in a strange vast space. Mommy is the only familiar
island in all directions. I know her by heart, but I want to
see what's around us. So I circle her farthest edges. I stay
in contact with her by touch, by smell, by memory, without
looking. I follow her contours to get different views outward. I am gently being called out and away from her. But
I linger on her shores to make a mind chart in which she
is the sure point at the very center. The pull outward grows.*

*I am now ready to break contact with her. I step off into
free space. At first, it takes my breath away. I float, swaying*

*freely. Then I can breathe again. I look back at her across the gulf before I start to move. Slowly I edge away. But I navigate by Mommy's presence. When I look back to see her across the gulf, she is the star I steer by. Even when I don't look at her, she sends curved lines of force flowing out into space. I can move along her rays of attraction.*

*Now I am farther out in space, coasting. I design turns and sweeps. I balance forces to make stops. I command and propel starts. I ride my own movements. Then I lose control over them, and they ride me. My movements and I take turns leading. But always as I move, the visible star and the invisible lines of force hold me steady in my wandering.*

*I approach people and pass around them. They bend space as my mother does, but in the opposite direction. They send out invisible lines of force that hold me away and guide me around them. I slip past them without even coming close.*

*Now I see something different. Another baby—one like me—is journeying out. She has the same special vitality I feel. But she doesn't bend the space at all, there's no push away. I am free to come close and explore and touch. Suddenly someone picks her up and sweeps her away.*

*And suddenly I am lost. I can't find Mommy's star, and her lines of force have grown weak. The space grows bigger and bigger. It becomes boundless. Nothing holds me. I am dissolving like grains of salt in the ocean of space. I panic.*

*I call to her. She is somewhere close, but I can't see her. I can vaguely feel her pull, but I can't touch her. Again, I throw out a cry, aiming blindly to catch hold of one of her invisible lines of force. My cry catches hold. I hear and feel her answering tug. Her call back is a hammer blow on a block of clear ice. The blow leaves a lacy pattern whose white fault lines and planes restructure the space. And like*

*that, my world is transformed by her voice. Using the
pattern of this new map, I can find my way back to the
point of the hammer blow, to her voice, to her.*

*Back with her again, at the sure point, my panic subsides
along the skin of my chest and neck. The quieting starts at
the surface and flows inward. In the wake of the quieting,
I find myself again. The pull of her presence gathers me up
out of space. I find my separateness again along the lines of
her touch.*

*I feel the calming sink in. But slowly I become aware,
anew, of the huge spaces surrounding us. Faintly, I hear
them call me forth again.*

—— ✖ ——

An infant feels tied physically and psychologically to her
mother. This bond, one of the more obvious and necessary
parts of an infant's social life with her parents, becomes
distinctly evident after the baby starts to walk. Joey, who
has been walking for a month, can now walk away from
his mother—unsteadily, to be sure—and walk or hurry on
all fours back to her. The force that pulls him back to his
mother, and keeps him close to her, we call the *attachment
system.* Countering this attachment system is Joey's curiosity
about the world, which pulls him into the environment to
explore it. We call this the *exploratory system.*

Joey is caught between the two systems, which often
compete with each other. When he has wandered too far
from his mother, or is in an unfamiliar place, as here in the
waiting room, his attachment system is activated, and he
stays closer to her. Close to her, he starts to feel secure, and
his attachment system is lulled. Then he is susceptible to the
attractions of the world beyond her. As they activate his

exploratory system, off he will go on a short voyage of exploration. It will last until for some reason, such as wandering too far, his attachment system again becomes activated and overrides the exploratory system, and back he comes.

Both tendencies in Joey are absolutely essential. He needs something to draw him into the world. Without the push of his own curiosity and desire to explore, he would never leave his mother's side and would learn nothing of the outside world on his own. But he also needs the opposite tendency, an inner pull to seek out, go toward, and cling to his mother. Without that, he would have less protection from external dangers, no means of getting found if lost, and no "haven of safety" with its feeling of security. With this as background, we can now pick up the story.

Joey finds himself in a "strange vast space" where his mother is "the only familiar island in all directions." The waiting room is totally new. It has no history. Immediately, his attachment system is turned on. His mother and her physical whereabouts become even more important than usual. Without any mental map to work with, Joey takes his bearings in this immense and unknown place.

When at home, Joey, now a year old, knows where things are—living room, bedroom, bathroom, and so on. And he knows what is likely to happen in these places. His attachment system is at rest in this familiar scene. But in this waiting room the only thing he knows is his mother. While he looks around, he makes certain he remains in physical contact with her. He slips off her lap onto the ground and slowly circles around her. First, he keeps his head against her knees. Then he keeps one hand turning around her legs like a maypole as he circles "her farthest edges," looking out. "I follow her contours to get different views outward."

Through this action, he accomplishes two goals. He is gaining the assurance to leave her and making an emotional-space map that will permit him to go. On this map his mother is at the emotional-geographic center. She is the only point of reference, his "sure point," and on it Joey measures distance according to his feelings of safety and fear.

After hovering around her for a while, Joey's need for attachment has been lowered enough that he starts to feel more strongly both the pull of his curiosity and the push of his desire to explore. Finally, they win out—just enough for him to take a first, tentative step away from his mother, out into the room, all alone. This first step must make a strong impression on him, even though he has done it before in other places. Each first time in a new place is risky but exciting. After all, he has let go his physical contact with his mother, and touching is the bedrock of attachment. His initial reaction to breaking contact with her and stepping off into "free space" is to feel stunned and disoriented: his breathing changes, and his balance is shaky; he floats, "swaying freely." Infants often give this impression of being momentarily shocked by the consequences of a step they have taken. Looking back at his mother, Joey regains his equilibrium and so can continue outward.

As Joey journeys into the waiting room, he keeps his mother's whereabouts much in mind. He frequently looks around to check that she is still there. Seeing her measures only the change in physical distance between him and her and her position in space. Joey also, as he moves, experiences changes in *emotional distance*. Recall for a moment your childhood and one of those games of tag where there was a "safe base." You would edge away from the "safe base" one step, two steps, teasing and challenging the child who was "it" to catch or touch you before you could get back to the home base. As, at each step farther away from the home base, the danger and excitement mounted, the emotional distance increased. For Joey in this situation, his mother must operate like a huge magnet: his emotional distance is measured by its pull, not in feet and inches, or in how much time it takes to get from here to there. This emotional distance is determined by the presence of his mother, "the star I steer by" as if space were thicker and more concentrated around her and thinner as he moves away.

When he's several yards away but in his mother's direct sight and presence, Joey feels secure enough to concentrate on his movements for their own sake. After all, his recent achievement of walking is still an enthralling activity requiring concentration and conscious effort. As the commander of these new emotions, his feeling of mastery and inventiveness must be intense: "I design turns and sweeps. I balance forces to make stops. I command and propel starts." But this process is still risky and uncertain. He is an inexperienced commander. His motions also get away from him: "I ride my own movements. Then I lose control over them, and they ride me." As his movements and he "take turns leading," he becomes his own rollercoaster.

As Joey moves about the waiting room, roughly in circles around his mother, and in her eyesight, he encounters strange adults. Since he was eight months old, he has been having negative reactions to strangers. In their presence, or especially when one approached him, he would stop whatever he was doing, watch that person vigilantly, become wary, and check to see whether his mother was nearby and that everything was O.K. A stranger who came too close would make him a little fearful. Beginning at that age, he started to divide the world sharply into two camps, strangers and familiars.

At the age of twelve months, in the waiting room, he manifests a new version of this *stranger reaction*. Now that he can move about, strangers and familiars create a different kind of emotional space around themselves. Familiar people like his mother set up a local psychological field of attraction, "a bend in space." Strangers create a psychological field of repulsion which Joey feels as holding him away, enabling him to slip past them without touching or "even coming close."

The little girl is a different story. She is not a familiar and yet not a stranger. Beginning at about three months of age, Joey has been able easily to distinguish between a baby and an adult, or even an older child. We are not sure how infants do it, but this ability seems to be based on the fact that adults and children generally have differently proportioned head and body sizes: that is, the younger a person, the bigger the forehead and the head, the larger the eyes, the smaller the nose and chin, in comparison with the size of the body. Infants are also expert, or as good as or better than adults, at distinguishing girl babies from boy babies. It appears that girls and boys, even when very young, have on the average slightly different facial configurations (granted, with much overlap). Visual discrimination experiments have suggested that babies are sensitive to these group differences.

Beginning at about three months, infants show an especially lively interest in all children, as if recognizing their own "species." Thus, the little girl Joey sees "has the same special vitality I feel." At eight months, strange children are largely spared the stranger reaction. (Presumably, it evolved to protect infants from strange adults who could do them harm; strange babies do not pose the same threat.) At twelve months, unknown children are not simply freely approachable ("she doesn't bend the space at all, there's no push away") but also create a special curiosity. Joey feels no constraint in walking right up to this girl and touching her, even on the face, in a kind of primordial freedom of intimacy. That is why the little girl's mother snatches her away. She is not sure what Joey will do.

In wandering away, Joey has been absorbed in the little girl. When he looks around to relocate his mother, he does not see her and is not sure where to look for her. He is, indeed, "lost" from his point of view. If he cannot see her star, he is lost; and if he cannot feel her invisible lines of force, he is "separated." Separation loss (even momentary) is probably the most anguishing experience a year-old child can have. Such moments demonstrate how a child's basic well-being and ordinary smooth functioning are dependent upon the sustaining presence of the primary caregiver. She is a psychological oxygen, without which, within seconds, the child experiences panic. And part of the panic of separation is most likely a feeling of becoming fragmented, of losing boundaries, of disappearing into a lonely, empty infinity. That is why Joey feels the space growing "bigger and bigger." "It becomes boundless. Nothing holds me. I am dissolving like grains of salt in the ocean of space."

These feelings are also a significant part of adult life. Adults with a fear of open spaces *(agoraphobia)* and panic attacks are thought by many psychiatrists to be suffering from an acute adult separation reaction. Almost anyone would panic at finding himself swimming in the ocean, out of sight of land, the boat drifting away. It would be like being alone in outer space if you weren't specially prepared for it by training and constitution. Even in ordinary life, the threat of separation from our most important partner—whether husband, wife, or parent—has similar, if less dramatic, effects. The separation reaction is basic to us all and may not change much from the age of twelve months till death. Certainly, we become better at avoiding it, at coping with it, and, perhaps most commonly, at designing our lives so that crucial separations are less of a potential threat. But they are always with us.

In his panic at being separated from her, Joey calls out to his mother, a cry he throws out like a lifeline in a blinding storm. Wherever she is, he hopes she catches it. Thus, her call in response to his is like an "answering tug." Once he hears her voice, he can start to undo the panic. He establishes coordinates of space around both "the hammer blow" of her call, "her voice," and her presence. And once reoriented in space, he returns to her.

Joey's mother runs to him as he runs to her. In fact, she has had him in view all the time and goes to him when she sees him get upset: she was lost to Joey, not the reverse. She picks him up and holds him against her chest, his head nestled in the crook of her neck and one of his arms around her neck. There he cries, more and more softly. The ultimate magic of attachment is touch. And this magic enters through the skin. For all primates—monkeys, chimps, humans—the final position for establishing or maintaining attachment is ventral contact (chest against chest, head upon the other's shoulder and neck). As Joey experiences it, "the quieting starts at the surface and flows inward."

Being held against his mother's body does more than just quiet Joey. The "pull of her presence" helps him to reconstitute and integrate himself after feeling "dissolved." Not only is he is soothed and reconstituted, but in fact, after that dissolution, he renews his separateness "along the lines of her touch."

Slowly, Joey's charged-up attachment system is deactivated. And as it subsides, his exploratory system begins to assert itself again, and his curiosity to re-emerge. Despite the perils of his grand voyage outbound, he will soon be ready to set forth again.

# 8

*A Shared Feeling:*

*11:50 A.M.*

*J*OEY and his mother are now back at home. They are looking for a stuffed rabbit, his favorite toy, which got hidden under a blanket. Joey finds it. He swings it excitedly into view and looks to his mother with a burst of pleasure. In a smooth crescendo, his face opens up. His eyes grow wider, and his mouth eases into a broad smile, to show her what he found—even more important, to show her how he feels about it. After she sees his face, he lets his face fall back to normal in a smooth diminuendo. She then says "YeaaAAaah!" with a rising, then falling pitch. Joey seems content with her response and goes on playing by himself.

*I found it! Here!*

*A wave of delight rises high in me. It swells to a crest. It leans forward, curls, and breaks into musical foam. The*

*foam slips back as the wave passes, and disappears into the*
*quieter water behind.*
   *Does she feel the wave too?*
   *Yes!*
   *She calls back the rising and falling echo of my wave. I*
*ride her echo up and down. It passes through me, and I sense*
*my delight in her.*
   *It now belongs to both of us.*

———— ❧ ————

This moment between Joey and his mother seems simple,
almost too ordinary and fleeting for anything of importance
to occur. Nonetheless, this moment provides a gateway to
the world of mutual mindscapes, to intersubjectivity. Here
is why.

During the past few months, Joey's mother has gradually
intuited, without being aware of it, that Joey has discovered
intersubjectivity, as I discussed in my introduction to this
part. He has come to realize that he can have feelings or
intentions, and that other people can not only know about
them but even share the same feelings or intentions with
him. He is also coming to realize that others can remain
unaware of what is going on in him, or that they may be
aware that something is going on, but not understand what
it is.

In this moment Joey is delighted to find the hidden toy.
His delight is the inner feeling that he may be able to share
with his mother. This feeling is the real subject of this
moment. Let us look closely at his delight. It occurs in two
different "places" simultaneously—one visible, the other
invisible. The visible events occur in Joey's face and eyes,
which open up and close back down in one smooth motion,

all in a moment. And Joey is careful to show these events to his mother, as a sign.

The invisible events are those inner sensations of delight that reside somewhere else in the body and mind than on the face. Joey can identify that place no better or worse than we can as adults. It is somewhere "inside." And what happens "inside," during a feeling, is an alive event which takes time to unfold. It is not static like a picture. It is not abstract like an idea. It is multiple shifting impressions that change all the time, as does music or dance. For instance, Joey first senses his feeling of delight surging in a crescendo as a wave rises and crests. At the high point or climax, his feeling "leans forward, curls, and breaks into a musical foam." Then, subsiding in a diminuendo, his feeling drops and disappears.

It is through this inner emotional choreography, or orchestration, that one experiences feelings at any age; indeed, in this respect, babies and adults probably do not differ much. Feelings unfold in time. They have a story line. They come, and stay awhile, even a split second, and leave. Feelings can arrive or depart with explosive suddenness (surprise at a sharp sound) or a gradual fading in or out (contentment). Their peak of intensity can be instantaneous (understanding the punchline of a joke) or a long flat plateau (slow-burning anger). Their entire presence may be low- or high-keyed. The lived experience of a feeling results not only from the sensation itself, but from how it is contoured and sequenced in time—like music. Thus, Joey's delight is being played out on his inner stage.

Now, it is only through his face that Joey's mother can glimpse the internal ballet of his subjective feelings. The face is the most extraordinary organ for the display of emotional events. Its many dozens of different muscles express a multiplicity of feelings and their nuances. That is as true for Joey at twelve months as it is for us as adults. The face acts something like a shadow screen on which is cast the inner drama of a human being. In fact, the same "forces" simultaneously direct the movements of the facial muscles and the dance of inner subjective feeling.

As Joey's delight surges within him and rises to a crest, his eyes and mouth open wider and wider in synchronization with the rise of his feeling. His breathing is also recruited into the flow. As the inner feeling reaches its peak and subsides, Joey exhales, and his face and eyes close back to their resting position again, synchronized with the passing of the feelings. During the diminuendo and release, he tightens his vocal cords, braking the escape of air and thus prolonging the fall of his facial expression to match the speed of the fading of the feeling. Joey's putting vocal brakes on the outflow of air makes a pleasing sound, the "musical foam" the wave breaks into. The opening and closing, or rising and falling, of Joey's facial expression corresponds exactly in duration and form with the surging and fading of the inner feeling.

Joey has a vague sense of all this. He is aware that his mother may be able to perceive his feeling, and that his face provides the means of her thus "reading" him. And he wants very much to be read. He probably experiences his desire to communicate his feelings as arising unseen from the inner feeling itself, to be sent out through him to reach his mother.

And now comes what is probably the most extraordinary part of this moment. Joey's mother has seen his face rise and fall with delight. She also knows the reason for it: his finding the lost toy and showing it to her. Like any parent, she wants to share his delight with him, to let him know that she knows what he has experienced, that she knows how he feels at that moment. What can she do to accomplish this?

She could say, "Oh, Joey, I know you felt delighted. I, too, know what that feels like." While Joey might understand some of these words, he doesn't yet understand this expression of the concept. What else could she do? Perhaps she could imitate him. That requires no language. By imitating what he did, she could try to show him that she understands what he must have felt like. But this wouldn't work either. If Joey's mother raised her empty hand into view, just as Joey did, and opened and closed her face in a faithful imitation of Joey's display of delight, it would look ridiculous. More to the point, what would Joey make of it? He might think, "O.K., you know what it was like to do what I did—after all, you imitated me faithfully. But can I be sure you really know what it felt like to be me when I did that? How do I know you're not a mirror? How do I know you even have a mind? In fact, how do I know you have feelings at all, or feelings anything like mine?" In short, faithful imitations will not do. So what can she do in this dilemma?

What she did do was say, "YeaaAAaah!" and, with her vocal pitch, imitated Joey's inner feeling, the rising and falling wave. She also carefully imitated the duration and temporal contouring of the crescendo–diminuendo. The rise in pitch of the first part of her "YeaaAA . . ." lasted exactly as long as the crescendo of Joey's face opening. Likewise, the fall in pitch of its last part lasted only as long as his face fall did. Avoiding a faithful imitation, she intuitively created the carefully selected and elaborated imitation that has been called *attunement*. She took those parts of what Joey did that best reflected his inner feeling—the rise and fall shape and its time course—and altered those parts that were specific to his modality of expression. She substituted a pitch change for a featural change, a facial expression for a vocal one. By succeeding in speaking to Joey's inner feeling while doing an end run around his overt behavior, she cannot be confused with a mirror. Only a human who knows what Joey felt could come up with a "YeaaAAaah" that is an analogue and not a copy of his experience. He understands that his message got to her, and answers "Yes!" This kind of analogic matching is done out of awareness, as a special manifestation of empathy. Most of us do it intuitively. And the child of a parent who, for whatever reason, cannot do this, or is inhibited from doing it, will feel psychically more alone with that person and perhaps ultimately in the world.

Letting her "YeaaAAaah!" travel through him ("I ride her echo up and down") to see whether it corresponds to the inner feeling he has just had, Joey perceives that she shares his feeling. He knows that her vocal response corresponds to his feeling because, as I discussed in chapter 3, he can translate from one sensory modality to another. He knows that a rising and a falling wave form in voice pitch is the same as a rising and a falling wave form in another person's face or in a feeling tone experienced somewhere inside himself. He thus recognizes the authenticity of his mother's response.

In this important moment, Joey and his mother have shared a feeling. However simple that may seem for an adult (it is not always), it is a big step for Joey. When he has a feeling inside, how is he to know whether he is the only person on earth to have ever felt it, or even something like it? And of all the ways he feels, how is he to know which can be shared with other people—or which should be kept private, even darkly secret? Which will be validated by others, some day to be named and talked about? The implication of these events is great. Such sharing is the basis for later aspects of psychic intimacy. How deeply can and should inner worlds be shown and shared? The depth of psychic intimacy with which Joey will ultimately feel comfortable is being established.

Joey and his mother are in the process of deciding the boundaries of the sharable universe of feelings. Together they have just established that a burst of delight is an inner event they can share: "It now belongs to both of us." But what about sadness, anger, pride, enthusiasm, fear, doubt, shame, joy, love, desire, pain, boredom? Still to come in Joey's life are experiences of these and other subjective states. Will Joey's mother be fully able to share them, or will she be unable, consciously or unconsciously, to let these feelings become full members of the universe Joey can later expect to share with others?

As Joey's mother and father thus let him know which mindscapes of his they can share and which not, they are beginning to shape him from the inside to become the son they have dreamed of. But if parents are not united in the important things they want in a child, he is unlikely to become the product of two incompatible dreams. He may then spend much of his life trying to resolve these contradictions within himself, or feel compelled by their tension to reject aspects of one of his parents—and thus himself.

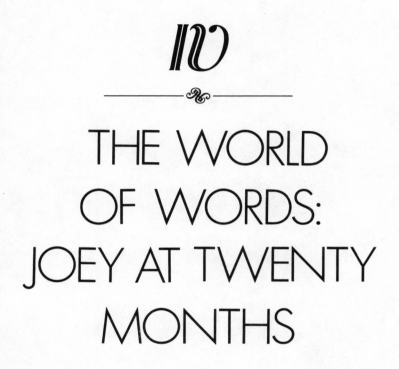

# THE WORLD
# OF WORDS:
# JOEY AT TWENTY
# MONTHS

AS Joey approached eighteen months, he began another major maturational leap that profoundly changed his daily experience: the leap into the world of words, of symbols and self-reflection. Joey is still in the middle of this leap. In some children it starts earlier; in some, later. The normal range is broad. We don't really know why this leap happens exactly when it does. The capacity for language and symbolization built into the human genes lies dormant until this age. The child who has had a reasonably average life experience will suddenly make a great advance in understanding language and slightly later will start to produce it. Like the unfolding of a flower, a uniquely human one, language blossoms overnight, when the time is right.

It is not only language, however, that comes suddenly into bloom. An entire garden of abilities springs up at this season of a child's life. Although the same conditions are needed for all of them, the arrival of language marks a traditional shift from infancy to childhood (hereafter, I will refer to Joey as a child). All of the abilities that emerge at this age are related. Children now begin to play out events—past, present, or future—on the stage of the mind. They can practice or reproduce or imagine events on the mental stage alone, before or without ever doing them in reality. And they now begin to use symbols and signs to refer to things and people. They can even refer to themselves.

Beginning now, Joey may observe someone do something he himself has never done before, such as dial a telephone or pour milk into a cup. Later that same day, or several days later, Joey will imitate the dialing or pouring for the first time in his life. To do this, he must have made and kept in his mind a model of the activity. And he must use that mental model to instruct himself how to do the dialing or pouring. Thus, he retains and then reproduces events on a mental stage. This is called *deferred imitation.*

Or, by combining symbolic events into new combinations, Joey can now create a desired mental scenario of events that never happened—or perhaps never will, such as flying by himself in a toy airplane to grandpa's house. Through his imagination, he can now symbolically enact his wishes; he is not bound to reality.

Joey's new behavior in front of a mirror is a good example of his new ability to see himself from the outside. After about eighteen months, if someone surreptitiously puts a spot of rouge on Joey's forehead so that he doesn't notice it, and then places him in front of a mirror so that he can see himself, he will immediately and without hesitation point his finger to the red spot on his real forehead. Before eighteen months, he would have pointed to the red mark on the forehead of his image in the mirror. Then he would not yet have understood that the mirror image stood for, or referred to, the real him. He now has this understanding.

And, finally, there has sprouted language, the most eye-catching flower in this garden. Joey now uses words as symbols to refer to persons, actions, and objects ("Mommy go bed"). Joey's use of the pronouns ("me, my, mine") as well as of his own name, "Joey," shows that he has also understood that he can refer even to himself.

Language opens up whole new worlds to Joey. The realization that he can unlock and use words must be like the feeling during the instant you realize that now you know how to ride a bike, or swim, or drive a car, or walk—or maybe the full force of all of them combined. But the feeling does not last only an instant. For Joey this exhilarating "instant" must stretch out over months, with ever-gathering force. Vistas must appear to open up without limit, as he is now able to go to places unimagined before, farther back into the past or ahead into the future, and to places that you can't get to without the steps and spring-boards of words strung together. Also, he can go to most of these new places with another person, by way of conversations and dialogues. This trip within a trip is a new and far-reaching way to be with another person. While language certainly gives Joey a new means of independence and freedom, it also provides him with the most potent means that exists to join with others and with the whole culture.

Language also radically changes Joey's world by restructuring it. It divides nonverbal experience into different and sharper categories. It marks the time line of events clearly into past, present, and future. It allows a wider network of associations. It transcends reality with greater ease. It stands outside the lived experience it reflects, as something separate that can be viewed and reviewed. I have tried to show the thrill of this bright side of learning language in chapter 9.

But there is also a dark side to language. It has enormous disadvantages, especially compared with the nonverbal system already smoothly functioning in Joey. Words cannot handle global experiences well. Language is ideally designed to make sharp categorical distinctions between things *(big, small)*, but is clumsy at noting gradations between its categories. Gestures help to indicate these gradations: to say something is "that big," for example, and spread your hands apart in a rough approximation of the size you mean. Language is slow. Action—expression and gesture—is fast. Language may split thought away from emotion. It breaks apart rich, complicated global experiences into relatively impoverished component parts. And, most important, some nonverbal experiences (like looking into someone's eyes while he or she is looking into yours) can simply never be captured in words: at best, they can be evoked by words. So when language comes into Joey's life, it creates a wide gulf between his familiar nonverbal world of experience and the new world of words. This schism is confusing and at times painful. For the first time in his young life, he has to hold onto two different versions of the same event. Life will now, and forever, be lived more in parallel. The simple wholeness of experience has been broken. How Joey lives this lonelier side of the advent of language is illustrated in chapter 10, which occurs on the same morning as chapter 9. From here on, for Joey, the verbal and the nonverbal constructions of experience will live together all the time.

# 9

## "Pumpkin":
## 7:05 A.M.

*J*OEY wakes up and gets out of bed. He stands looking about for a moment, as if thinking. He then goes quickly into his parents' bedroom and gets into their bed. He slips under the covers, between them, burrowing deep. His parents are pretty much awake by now. After a while, his father says to him, "My little pumpkin?" Joey answers back from under the covers, "Umpin." His father gently corrects, "Yes, pumpkin." Joey tries it again: "Pumpkin." His father laughs, "That's it, you're my little pumpkin."

Joey is quiet for a while. Then he comes out from the covers and announces clearly and firmly, "Me pumpkin!"

— ❧ —

*My room is so still. I am all alone here. I want to go where Mommy and Daddy are. If I don't go, I will stay alone and still. So I go to their room, and get in between them, into that valley. There, I wrap myself in the heat that rises and falls. I immerse myself in the pools of warm smells, in the sounds of air flowing in and out of them as the valley fills and empties. I bathe in the rich tides of our morning world.*

*Then Daddy sends into my world a familiar sound—just for me. Its music unlocks the warm Daddy-feeling. For the first time, I notice that the sound has a special shape, one that stands apart from its music. This shape is bright and soft and lingers after the music is gone. It has a force and life of its own. It was hiding in the flow of the music but has come out. I can play with this brand-new shape. It has curves with little explosions. I try it and send it to Daddy. He sends it back to me, clean and sharp. I am getting it now. I send it back. He laughs and sends it to me again, this time flowing free and full.*

*This new shape takes me into myself. There the shape unfolds by itself but also emerges from inside me. It grows and spreads. I let it fall over and around me. I press it close against my feelings.*

*Now I'm ready. I rise up wrapped in my new shape. That bright, soft cloak changes me. I fling myself out of the valley and declare myself: "Me pumpkin!"*

———— ✄ ————

Joey's feeling of loneliness upon waking up this morning is different from the acute anxiety of separation last year (see chapter 7). Now he has some feeling of isolation, of being cut off from human contact. He misses being surrounded by human life, and knows all that activity is going on somewhere. It is the inanimate, nonhuman aspect of his room that most upsets him: "It is so still." Also, Joey now has a fair grasp of the immediate future and of the past, and makes predictions: "If I don't go, I will stay alone and still. So I go to their room." He grasps the concepts, but not yet the verbal meaning, of *if* and *so* and *because.*

Knowing exactly where to go to find human life in a concentrated form, he climbs into his parents' bed. Into the "valley" between them, he "wraps" and "immerses" and "bathes" himself in the smells, heat, motions, and sound of his parents' "morning world," in all its nonverbal sensations and feelings.

Here, in this valley, Joey has an important encounter with language. In discovering that a word or a phrase can stand for something else, he possesses the key that unlocks language. Usually around eighteen months of age, but sometimes later, babies find this key. Joey has already found the key with other words, such as *doggie, cat,* and *baba* (grandmother). Knowing the word that stands for and refers to those animals and people, Joey uses the same key to unlock other new words. Each first unlocking of a new word—today it is *pumpkin*—is a startling discovery. In the process, a child claims something new from the nonverbal flux.

It is into this flux that Joey's father throws a fragment of language: "My little pumpkin." Mostly so far, in respect to language, Joey has heard only its music. He hears the pure sound of the words and feels the emotions the sounds evoke in him, but he hears little of the strict meaning of the language. In other words, the fragments of language dissolve and become part of the nonverbal flux. Thus, when Joey's father called him by a pet name, the familiar sound— "its music"—"unlocks the warm Daddy-feeling."

But, for a change, on this particular morning, Joey's father's language does not vanish into music and feeling. Something "stands apart," and Joey recognizes it. This—the special meaning of the word and the person it refers to—is what Joey calls its "shape," which emerges from the music.

Once Joey has realized that "pumpkin" stands alone as a sort of sound-object, he can start to explore it and play with it: that is, he can find or provide its meaning. He must master the sound and keep it, not just let it wash over him like music. When he tries, he finds that "the sound has curves with little explosions." The *um* and *in* are the rounded sounds, the "curves"; and *p* and *k* are the explosive consonants ("plosives"). Joey's job is to get them together right. To do this, he and his father resort to something they learned long ago: they toss the word back and forth, making it better each time. The game and the rules of alternating turns have been used by Joey and his parents for many months. They used to take turns cooing to each other when he was only three months old. They rolled balls back and forth from the time he was seven months. The basic rules of conversation, turn taking, were long established before Joey and his parents even applied them to language. So, once again, Joey and his father follow these tried-and-true rules and send the word *pumpkin* back and forth between them. And Joey's father immediately capitalizes on this excellent teaching and learning format.

The first time Joey tries his turn, he leaves out the exploding consonants, and says, "Umpin." His father then does as most parents intuitively do in this situation: he slowly and clearly enunciates the not-yet-learned-parts of the word, "*P*ump-*K*in," and leaves unstressed the already-learned parts, "Umpin." Thus, to Joey, his father's response is "clean and sharp." Using this teaching technique, Joey quickly gets it right. When his father then says, "That's it, you're my little pumpkin" in his natural voice, Joey experiences his father sending the word back "free and full."

Joey now has hold of the word. He has to work on it and let it work on him. The surprise of his revelation accomplishes both goals by capturing his attention and centering it on the word itself: "This new shape takes me into myself." What happens now is truly wonderful. When a word is first unlocked, and its meaning released, the meaning is given to Joey from outside himself by someone else; at the same instant, he alone discovers and creates it. After all, his father first presented or gave the word *pumpkin* to Joey. It is his gift. Joey already has, however, something in his experience (himself as seen in the affectionate tie with his father) for the word to go with. It is Joey who discovers and creates the relation between the new word and his previous experiences: "It grows and spreads out. I let it fall over and around me. I press it close against my old feelings." In this sense, the word is, at the same time, given and found, a discovery and a creation that emerges in the mind: "There the shape unfolds by itself but also emerges from inside me."

Once Joey has worked on the word and let it work on him, it is his. He can now use the word to refer to a new aspect of himself within the context of his special relationship with his father: "I fling myself out of the valley and declare myself, "Me pumpkin!"

One last mystery. Joey has never heard "Me pumpkin" before. Perhaps no one has ever said it before. His father has said only, "Little pumpkin," "My little pumpkin," and so on. He has never said, "Me pumpkin," and it is not likely he ever would have. Thus, Joey is not imitating anybody. Instead, he has created for himself a meaning, by bringing together himself ("me"), a word sound (p.u.m.p.k.i.n.), and a special experience, a way of being loved and viewed by his father ("Me pumpkin").

This very small example of the massive task of restructuring experience from the nonverbal to the linguistic was pleasurable for Joey. But the restructuring process may encounter obstacles, as we will see in chapter 10.

# 10

# Worlds Collide:
# 7:21 A.M.

LATER on the same morning, when everyone is up, Joey is standing in his own room waiting to be dressed. His mother will be back in a minute. He sees the sunlight on his wall and floor. He walks over to a sunpatch lying on the dark wooden floor. Absorbed, he drops to his hands and knees. He looks at it. He touches it with his hand. He lowers his face and touches the sunpatch with his lips.

At that moment, his mother returns and sees him. She is both surprised and a little disgusted. She shouts, "Don't do that! Joey, what are you doing?" Joey stops abruptly. He stares at the spot of sunlight, then looks up at his mother. She walks over to him, bends down, puts her arm around him, and says reassuringly, even with a smile, "That's just sunshine, honey. It's just to look at. It's only light on the floor. You can't eat this sunshine. It's dirty."

Joey looks at her a long while and then back at the

sunpatch on the floor. He disengages himself from her arm and walks out of the room.

—— ✤ ——

*The morning glow is there again, with its slow dance on the wall. And on the floor it is a pool, bright and beautiful and deep. It is like looking down long stairs. It is warm, like a blanket. It vibrates like music, glows like honey. And it tastes like——*

*Mommy's voice slaps me. At once it freezes my bright space. It chills the warmth, stops the music, douses the glow. Why?*

*I search her face. I see it get all pinched around her nose. It turns quickly into anger. Then both expressions flow out together, and loving rushes in. I am still stunned. She holds me and says soft, lilting words. Yet each of her words is a muffled blow that cracks my space into pieces.*

*"Just sunshine"—but it was my pool, a special pool!*

*"It's just to look at"—I heard it. I felt it, too!*

*"Only light on the floor"—How?*

*"It's dirty"—I was in it.*

*When she stops, the pieces lie all around. That world is gone. I feel naked and sad. I'm all by myself.*

—— ✤ ——

Language can create new worlds, like the "me pumpkin" one in the previous chapter. It can also destroy worlds, as it does here.

As this moment begins, Joey sees his old friend the sunpatch; and it draws him into that global, nonverbal world of experience in mixed modalities which I have described before. It is this nonverbal world that risks being destroyed when it collides with the world of language.

When Joey encountered the sunpatch at six weeks of age (see chapter 1), everything occurred in the present. As adults we spend less time totally in the present moment. Our memories of past experiences are so rich and so easily evoked that the past almost inevitably enters into, enriches, and permits us to interpret the present. Or, the anticipated future can mix in the present as a fantasy. As a result, our subjective experience of the present is impure: a cloth of many colors whose weft is threads from the past and expectations for the future, its warp threads from the here and now.

No longer does Joey, now almost two years old, live in a simple present moment as he did at six weeks. Now his present is rich with past experiences. What has changed is the breadth and power of his recall memory, a memory that can be readily tapped by only a small hint. (When he goes to the pediatrician's office now to get his shots, he need only see a white coat, or smell the place, to start crying.) So Joey has all the capacities and abilities to experience a subjective present that is a patchwork of times and places as an adult's is. But does he experience the present this way?

I suspect that, at this moment of being alone and contemplating a sunpatch in a sort of reverie, his subjective experience is closer to ours, as adults, than to his at six weeks. His present experience is now, in large part, created and colored by the memory of his past experiences.

For Joey, "the morning glow" evokes his old and daily friend, the sunpatch on the wall with "its slow dance." He is most captivated, however, by the sun falling on the floor in "a pool." This pool—"bright, beautiful, and deep"—

exerts its charms on him in the here and now; it also evokes other nonverbal memories which surface to join and help form the present experience. The "pool" evokes great depths he must have experienced elsewhere, "like looking down long stairs." It evokes the warmth of a "blanket," which he must have felt often before. Its shimmering quality triggers the recall of musical vibrations, which are not part of the present scene. Its glow recalls the radiance of honey which he sees in a jar each morning. Joey's memory system is in full swing. Associations are being triggered, and memory traces activated—out of awareness, to be sure. But these activations, nonetheless, structure Joey's present experience.

To weave such a subjective tapestry, Joey must be able to associate one experience with another, across space and time. Until recently, it was thought that infants needed developed language or symbols not only to represent events but also to be able to associate these representations. It now seems that nonverbal, even global, experiences can also be remembered and represented without being transposed into words. And associations between these nonverbal representations can be made to form complex networks. Joey can now do that.

A nonverbal event, even though experienced globally as one single event, consists of different parts: how it smells, looks, feels, and so on. The smell of one experience can remind one of the smell of a past experience and, in doing so, can re-evoke the whole past experience. Symbols or words are not needed for this kind of associative networking, though they are for the resulting network to be clear and its various contributions identifiable. The tapestries adults make have clearer patterns and can be unraveled, their original threads sorted out. Joey's cannot be because they have never been verbalized.

So as Joey contemplates the sunpatch on the floor, mingling past and present, his mother walks in and finds him with his lips touching the floor. Shocked, she wants to stop him. Her cry "Don't do that!" is a thunderclap disrupting his reverie. Everything stops. Joey's reverie is drained of all its vividness, his bright world frozen. Joey does not know why this has happened, and searches her face for an explanation. There, he initially sees disgust and anger. In unexpected situations, people may show a sequence of split-second emotions. Her initial disgust at Joey's mouth touching the floor gives way to anger that he doesn't understand any better. Her anger then dissolves as she realizes that, of course, he doesn't, and that the situation is actually endearing and funny. Caring and compassion now fill her face. Joey, like any child, wholly follows the progression of her feelings, but none makes sense to him in the context of his immediate experience.

Now comes the most agonizing part of this moment. Joey's mother, recovered from her shock, tries to make it all right for him. She tries with language. And what happens? Without intending to do so at all, she progressively, almost systematically, further shatters his nonverbal, global world. Joey's reverie combines qualities in many different modalities—intensity, warmth, vibration, brightness; and its essence is that he is not expressly aware of it as a visual experience. Yet his mother makes him aware of exactly that. Her words ("just to *look* at . . . only a *light*") have separated out precisely those properties that anchor Joey's experience to the single modality of vision. In so doing, her words isolate the

visual mode from the global flux (feeling-hearing-touch-
ing-seeing) in which it was originally embedded, and
fracture that wholeness of Joey's global experience. "But
it was my pool! I heard it. I felt it, too."

Her next words ("It's only light on the floor. You
can't eat this sunshine") have a different impact on his
world. She is explaining and analyzing the situation.
Words can, at their best, do this like nothing else. To
explain and analyze, you have to step back from an experience. Joey was inside the experience, living it and not
looking at it. His mother's words force a distance between him and his experience. In going on to call the
sunshine "dirty," she further boils down his rich reverie,
the single act, into a "bad" category of that act. It has
become a forbidden act. Thus, each additional phrase of
hers further "cracks" Joey's world "into more pieces." Finally, they lie shattered all around him.

This kind of thing must happen every day, many times
a day, during this phase of Joey's life of rapidly learning
language. In these collisions of the world of language with
the nonverbal world, sometimes he will be able to jump
partly out of the nonverbal and embrace the verbal, as with
"me pumpkin," to create a new parallel world. At other
times, the nonverbal is too shattered for him to have a secure
place to jump from. Then he is nowhere. There is not
enough left in the old world to hold on to; and the new
world, where his mother stands at this moment, is distant
and alienating. He has lost one and not gained the other: "I
feel naked and sad. I'm all by myself."

Such moments are breaks in the intersubjectivity between
parent and child. In a momentary failure of empathy, the
mother fails to see the situation from Joey's perspective and

to come around to repair the break. It is important for parents to be aware of the potential for such breaks at this point in development when the child is struggling with learning a new code for old experiences. Especially so, when the ruptures are subtle and it is often hard to know what went wrong or why. Empathic caregivers can help the child knit together these two worlds.

*v*

# THE WORLD OF STORIES: JOEY AT FOUR YEARS

$\mathcal{A}$ROUND three or so years of age, a child takes another great leap in development, a leap that makes her into a "different" child, while still remaining herself. As during the other great leaps, developmental changes occur in almost all areas of Joey's experience. But there is one change that plays a special role in this diary. Finally, Joey can himself tell the story of the events and experiences that happen to him. He can now weave together an autobiographical narrative.

A narrative is not just having words for things, as Joey has had that since his second year. Narratives go further. They involve seeing and interpreting the world of human activities in terms of story plots. These stories are made up of actors who have desires and motives directed toward goals, and they take place in a historical context and physical setting that help to interpret the plot. Also, each story has a dramatic line, with beginning, middle, and end. One

131

builds up to, or winds down from, a high point of dramatic tension. In other words, Joey starts to see human activities, his own now included, in terms of psychological explanations embedded in the structure of a narrative.

Take this sequence of events: (1) A man is walking down a sidewalk. (2) He starts to cross the street. (3) A man and a woman holding hands are walking on the other side of the street, toward the place where he will arrive on the sidewalk. (4) He stops in the middle of the street, (5) hesitates, and (6) returns to his side of the street. (7) He continues walking. An adult finds it almost impossible not to read into this sequence a story, that is, a psychological explanation of the events in terms of actors, motives, goals, contexts, and a dramatic line that rises and falls. Of course, many stories (that is, psychological interpretations or explanations) are possible. The woman on the other sidewalk could be the first man's wife. Or, he could owe the other man money and not want to be confronted by him. Or, the first man could be a spy secretly visiting this city who recognizes the couple on the other side of the street and knows they could give him away. And so on.

The point is that the mind integrates the man's separate actions into a single story plot. A possibility here could be: "A man unexpectedly saw—in fact, almost bumped into—his wife holding hands with another man. Shocked, he changed directions to avoid them and kept going as if nothing had happened, so he could collect himself and think." The seven separate actions observed fall into the background, where they act merely as clues upon which to hang a plot. And rushing into the foreground, the story defines what one has observed—what has "happened."

To understand human activities in terms of psychological story plots is part of the huge leap Joey is now making.

Beginning now, and for the rest of his life, he will comprehend human events largely as psychological stories—simple ones, at first.

This transformation in Joey's world view of human actions is not unique to him. All children, roughly between two and a half and four years of age, start to comprehend and make up narratives about their own lives. Also, adults of all cultures express their history, beliefs, values, and practices in the form of stories as psychological narratives. These stories are among a culture's most potent forms of self-expression and among its most effective forces for perpetuating itself.

Because story making (and story telling) is both common to all cultures, and an expected developmental landmark for all children, we now think of story making as a universal human capacity. It is a developmental landmark similar in many ways to sitting up, learning to walk, or acquiring speech. Like those capacities, story making unfolds according to a genetically determined timetable. Of course, important environmental factors determine the exact time of its appearance and how fully or richly it is employed.

The human mind seems naturally to seek explanations for what happens to us and around us. The pieces of our extremely diverse lived experience are but loosely connected, and the connections we impose often merely circumstantial or even accidental. The human mind needs to select meaningful details out of this disarray and pull them together into the most coherent, comprehensive, consistent, commonsensical, and simple organization possible. The story is one way of making that organization. It is the result of the mind's constant and restless search for order, for the "larger picture." Although this search begins at birth, until about three or four years of age Joey has had a limited capacity to create a large picture from his diverse experiences. He could do it only for small pieces of experience. Now, in this developmental leap, he has acquired the mental abilities and conceptions to combine in a unit, a story, enough pieces whose connection with one another makes sense of particular human events. The story plot becomes for the rest of our lives the basic "unit" for understanding the human events that affect us.

When you read Joey's story as he tells it—as opposed to his experience of the event—a major question about his story making arises. Where does the material for it come from? Past experiences, recalled from his memory, are a major source. But if those were the only source, the stories would be limited to what has really happened to him—as remembered or reinterpreted in the present. How, then, can Joey have an imaginary lion living on his wall, and go fishing from the bed, as he does in his diary in chapter 11?

Joey's stories, and everyone else's, transcend the actual, and become something else, for several reasons. First, Joey can mix together the memories of events that occurred at different times and places. Some of his stories activate memories from both the near past and the far and bring them all together in the present as if they were integral parts of the same story line. Second, some of the events that get mixed into the story can be imaginary or "pretend," like his lion. (Imaginary events also, of course, have some history in actual past experience.) Third, there is the structure of a narrative. Joey must force his diffuse and rich subjective experiences into the strict form a narrative requires. It is often hard to fit the unruly material of direct subjective experience into the ordered elements of a story. Much material gets left out, and other material gets reshaped to fit better. Finally, a story is told to someone else and will be adjusted to the listener. The teller must assume a stance relative to the material and the audience. Some stories require several versions.

Thus, by creating a story, Joey is creating a new reality. He now has two realities to live with: as lived subjective experience, and as narrated in a story. While related, these two worlds are not the same; they coexist.

To show these two worlds, Joey's diary entry describes, as it has all along, the world of his direct subjective experiences during a morning. An hour afterward, he narrates to me his story about the same morning experiences. The juxtaposition of these two worlds will demonstrate how a child takes the material of the subjectively experienced world and transforms it into a story world.

The nature of Joey's direct subjective experience has also changed. It is adultlike in that he associates more freely from one event to another regardless of when or where the events took place or whether they are real or imaginary. Often, perhaps always, two or more things are going on simultaneously. His associations range across time, space, and logic, so that he lives in extremely rich streams of consciousness. Events in time present, from the near past, and from Joey's far past can all activate one another and flow together to make up his direct subjective experience. Joey is as comfortable with the richness and unruliness of his streams of subjective experience as all of us are, or should be. That is how the mind works, especially when running relatively free, whether you are four years old or an adult.

I also assume that Joey has access to memories from his early past, like the experience of the sunpatch on his wall. I do not mean that he actually remembers a particular act of looking at the sun on the wall. Rather, the feeling it evoked in him with its associations is a category of experience that can recur and has often done so. It can be activated because he has frequently re-experienced it in his life in various contexts. It is a category of memories that has been reworked and kept active. Memories from the far past that are not selected for use (reactivated and recontextualized) tend to fade (perhaps never totally) and become a less available part of the mental landscape. If frequently used and updated, they remain highly available.

Joey's task of story making is to narrate to me the flow of his experience. As he does that, he is not simply creating a different and alternative version of what happened; he is creating a version that may well become the "official," public version. Stories about the past, by selecting from the many events one has directly experienced, have the power to define for each of us what "really happened." In this sense, Joey is participating in the extraordinary, daily pursuit of creating his past.

What happens if the lived past and the narrated past are very discrepant or contradictory? It is significant in this connection that stories, especially "official stories" of the past, are usually constructed by the child with the "help" (participation) of a parent. They are co-constructions. A child who has been physically abused may, for example, narrate a story excusing her parents: "They beat me because they care so much about me and what I do." But while this story may keep outsiders from confronting the parents with their abuse and thus save the child from a beating, the danger is that she may come to believe it: the story may become what she accepts as true of herself. Or, suppose a girl narrates that "my mother is the most loving and fun of all mothers. She plays with me all the time. We play house and . . ." Yet at the same time, the girl experiences her mother as too involved, as playing for herself, not for her daughter, as sometimes lost in her own world when they play together. It may be too painful or confusing for this girl to elaborate a "truer" story. Or, a father's eyes may light up when he looks at his oldest son and dim when he looks at his youngest; but the youngest narrates a second hand story that has become his own story: "My father loves us the same. He even says so all the time." Thus, story making can establish and perpetuate distortions of reality—distortions that contribute significantly to mental disturbance. Indeed, much of psychotherapy is concerned with unearthing and carefully describing a person's lived subjective and narrated worlds, then comparing the two, and finally bringing them into some degree of harmonious coexistence by altering one or both—usually the world of stories.

In normal development, however, story making has the important role of facilitating the daily process of self-definition. The child, narrating an autobiographical story, is not only defining his past; he is creating his identity. This process goes on every day, many times: when he recounts what happened at nursery school, or what he had for breakfast, or shopping with Mommy, or the fight he just had with his sister. Each story making and story telling is like a workshop where he can experiment on becoming himself. This is crucial for a child who is rapidly changing—that is, developing and maturing. His identity changes, too. And he must experiment with several versions, ranging from the public to the very private.

In chapter 11, Joey enters this dynamic world where he simultaneously discovers and creates himself. This is the last world into which we will follow Joey. Not because it is the last he will encounter in his life, but because after he has entered it, he will be able to construct and tell his own autobiographical tale without my aid.

# 11

## Parallel Worlds: 8:00 A.M. and 9:00 A.M.

*T*HIS morning's emotional context was set by the events of last evening, when family friends, along with their daughter, a little girl Joey's age, were visiting. He and the girl, Tina, got to pushing over a toy. He hit her, and her lip bled. Everyone was upset. Joey got sent to his room. And later, even the normal bedtime ritual was disturbed, and the bedtime song he and his mother usually sing was left unsung.

Now, the next morning, Joey wakes up. After waking, he lies in his bed musing a short while. Then he goes into his parents' room. They are just waking up, and all three of them play a "pretend" game on the bed. Then Joey goes into the kitchen with his mother, who prepares breakfast.

Joey's diary entries recording these three events as they occur—in his bed, in his parents' bed, in the kitchen— constitute his private subjective experience of them, just like all his other entries. The pieces that make up the patchwork of his subjective experience come from many sources and time periods, as I have indicated. To denote which these are in the three diary entries that follow, I have used three sets of symbols. Events from Joey's near past are surrounded by single parentheses, ( ). Events that come from his far past, and that have already been described earlier in his diary, are surrounded by double parentheses, (( )). Imaginary events are surrounded by brackets, [ ]. And everything that actually happens in the present is written normally and is unmarked. For Joey, of course, all these pieces are melded together into a single lived present.

About one hour after Joey has had these three experiences as they appear in his diary, I arrive to visit him and his parents, as I often do. He knows me well. I ask him, "What did you do this morning, Joey?" And he tells me.

His narrative of these same morning events does not emerge smoothly. Like most kids, Joey tells his story in bits and pieces. Since he needs some help, I prompt him with nondirective questions like "Oh?" or "And then?" Thus, his narrative is in the form of a dialogue.

I have broken this dialogue up, so that each of the three episodes of Joey's story follows the relevant diary entry—a juxtaposition that highlights Joey's work of transformation from the World of Experience to the World of Story. Together, these form the story version of his lived experiences, at least the version he is willing and able to tell me.

## IN MY BED

### *Joey's Diary*

*On my wall I watch my sunpatch. It feels good. ((The warm dance on the wall approaches.))*

*It is all yellow like the lion in my book. [The lion in the book wakes up slowly and yawns, and all his teeth show.]*

*(When Mommy makes like a lion, she moves in slow motion,) ((like the dance that flows on my wall.)) (She opens her mouth wide and wrinkles up her nose and yawns loud and rolls her head to the side and paws the air with her hand—as if she is contented with herself.)*

*She is not really a lion. With a real lion, all the other animals are afraid because he is the strongest.*

*(I hit Tina yesterday, 'cause she pushed me. And her lip got full of blood. She cried, and everyone turned and looked at me, as if I changed. And after, when I yelled at Mommy, Daddy whirled around and looked at me that same way, as if I changed.)*

*(I wanted to hide, to disappear far away. I was locked to a spot. My face burned, and everyone saw me. I couldn't escape, and I couldn't go to them. Then Mommy led me to my room and closed the door, leaving me alone. I cried and, after a while, sang real loud. I made music on the bed posts.) ((And somewhere was a slower, deeper rhythm.)) (I made like a cyclone with my toys.)*

*((Inside, everything was exploding out and then coming back to me.)) (Nobody came, and I got sad and lonelier.)*

*My sunpatch moves slowly, [like the lion just getting awake. My bed posts make a cage for him. Now he is cozy in his cage, and not so lonely. Are you, Lion?] So I can go now.*

## Joey's Story

D.S.: *What happened this morning, Joey?*

Joey: *I played. I played with my lion. He lives on my wall.*

D.S.: *Does he?*

Joey: *Yeah, and he's all yellow and big, BIG! But he is not bad. He's a good lion. My Mommy and Daddy don't want him out . . . so he hides behind my bed posts.* \*

D.S.: *Your bed posts?*

Joey: *My bed posts make a cage, and he moves in his cage, real slow, round and round. So slow, 'cause he's lonely. Yesterday he danced and sang and made music on the posts with his hands and on the wall, like it was a big drum, with his tail.*

D.S.: *Oh!*

Joey: *He sang a long song about when he was little, and about he was fighting, and there was a big storm and everything came apart and blew away. Yeah, and the song took a whole day till he was done. And then, then he went to sleep.*

D.S.: *Wow!*

Joey: *He doesn't sing when Mommy or Daddy come in.*

D.S.: *No?*

Joey: *No. You can only see him in the morning. But sometimes I can see him in the night when I want. He likes the morning best.*

---

\*The ellipses in Joey's story indicate where he paused in his narration.

## IN MOMMY AND DADDY'S BED

### Joey's Diary

*So I tiptoe to their bedroom.*
*They are a little asleep.*
*Maybe I can wake them, and not wake them, if I move*
*softly on the bed—like this.*
*[There are big waves on all sides, like mountains that roll*
*around. I am in my nutshell boat. I ride up the crest and*
*slide down the back of a wave, slipping sideways.] ((The*
*morning bed-tides make the air breathe. Sounds and smells*
*go away and come back.))*
*Daddy is really awake. He says, "Look out! Here comes*
*a big wave, a huge wave!" His leg rises up under the cover.*
*I am terrified with delight, [and the wave tumbles me into*
*the water] and under the covers. I am so happy they are all*
*awake. ((The world is warmer and faster.))*
*We are all laughing on the same bed. [We are all in the*
*same boat, and it is our house. I have to catch a fish from*
*the side to eat for breakfast.*
*I have a fish on my line. It is pulling and running and*
*skips out of the water. It is a special fish. It doesn't like to*
*be caught.]*
*(Once Daddy caught a huge fish, red-orange, and*
*brought it home, in the sink, and we ate it.)*
*[I go back into the dark cave on our boat.]*
*((Once he threw a magic sound into the dark cave to*
*catch a special fish, and it turned into a pumpkin, and I came*
*out of the cave,)) [and I come out of the cave,] and I come*
*out from under the covers, and Mommy and I go to the*
*kitchen.*

## Joey's Story

D.S.: And then what happened?

Joey: I went into Mommy and Daddy's room to play.

D.S.: And what happened there?

Joey: Well, they were asleep. So I played "nutshell."

D.S.: What's "nutshell"?

Joey: I have a nutshell. It can sail anywhere—in the tub or an ocean or a teacup. And I sail in my nutshell on the bed.

D.S.: Oh, and then?

Joey: See, Daddy was really pretend asleep. So then we all played "same boat" on the bed.

D.S.: How did you play "same boat"?

Joey: We live on our boat. And I almost caught a big fish.

D.S.: Oh!

Joey: Yeah. It pulled and pulled and ran away and came back. I could almost see it. I heard it. And it got away. It's a very special fish, it's . . . no one's ever caught it, maybe Daddy did once. It's called a pumpkin fish. I don't know, maybe it's round. And it can skip on top of the water. My friend JoJo can skip, and Marcie, but not Adele. She can't skip. And I'm learning. I never really saw a pumpkin fish, 'cause it gets away just at the end. So no one knows what it looks like. But it's a very special fish. So then, we didn't eat fish for breakfast. But sometimes we did.

## IN THE KITCHEN

### *Joey's Diary*

Now in the kitchen, we sing the unsung song from last night. *((Its sounds are alive inside me. They resurface, then slip back in,))* while she is making breakfast.

Her back is to me, so she doesn't see. She doesn't know that I know how. I pour cream in her coffee cup for her. She turns and sees me doing it. Her face stops. *((Might the wind die and the world be dead?))*

And then she explodes. She laughs and comes and hugs me and looks at me in the eye. In her eyes I feel her surprise. *[As she looks in, she replays the scene,]* and her surprise breaks into her eyes and over her face again in a second wave. *((I am passing deeper in. A new current is running up to the surface, softer in her eyes, far softer.))*

She laughs and pulls us back to here.

So here, I lift my hand to the sugar bowl and put one cube of sugar in her coffee. I wait a little. Then another. And I can't stop from laughing because I know that's right—two cubes.

And she laughs, too.

And we both laugh and laugh and laugh, *((running before the freshest and sweetest of all breezes.))*

## *Joey's Story*

D.S.: And then what happened?

Joey: At breakfast we laughed and we LAUGHED and LAUGHED... 'cause it was so funny. And we didn't stop laughing 'cause I surprised her.

D.S.: Oh?

Joey: See, I put one sugar in the coffee. And she watched. And then I put another sugar in. And she watched. And then I stopped 'cause two is all. And I poured cream in her coffee, too—when she didn't see me. So she turned around, and it was all done.

D.S.: And what else happened?

Joey: Well, . . . we sang the night song from last night, even at breakfast. . . . I can sing it?

D.S.: Yes.

Joey: It goes:

> In the four corners of the bed,
> are four bouquets of flowers.
>
> In the middle of the bed,
> the river is so deep.
>
> All the horses of the king
> could drink there together.
>
> And there we could sleep,
> and there we could sleep, yes,
> till the end of the world.

D.S.: That's beautiful.

*Joey:* Yeah.

*D.S.:* You sing that every night?

*Joey:* Yeah, Mommy and me, us both. We didn't sing it last night.

*D.S.:* Oh. And then what happened?

*Joey:* And then, . . . and then it's now. I'm talking to you.

———— ❧ ————

While, at first glance, Joey's diary entries (his experience world) and the story he recounted to me (his story world) are alternate views of the same life events, they are really "about" different things: they are two parallel worlds. Joey both experiences and constructs these worlds differently, and they serve different purposes.

The experience world is the present moment as it rolls forward in time. Never graspable, it is the dream being filmed. It is infinitely rich in sensations, perceptions, feelings, thoughts, actions. It becomes organized at the moment it is lived. The mind moves with great speed and smoothness across time and place, back and forth between memories, in and out of imaginary happening. Most experiences are simultaneous: we are sensing, while perceiving, while acting, while thinking, while feeling. Also, experience doesn't stop. It would appear that we live in the never-ending five-ring circus of our senses. Our attention, however, and our awareness, or consciousness, select and structure our ongoing lived experience to reduce the chaos. Accordingly, we feel as if we are moving along a single line, rather than on five or so parallel lines; and that life is a mainly linear, relatively continuous, partially coherent experience in time, rather than a totally fractured jumping from one ring to the next and back, or a cacophony of simultaneous experiences.

Processes of the mind, by making sense of Joey's experience world, enable it to hold together. At first, Joey appears to jump all over the place. In his bedroom, he goes from the sunpatch to the lion in a book, to his mother's imitation of a lion, to the dance of sunlight on the wall, back to his mother's imitation, off to lions in general, then to an incident that happened yesterday when he hit the little girl and was put in his room, then off on two side trips to older memory snatches, back to yesterday's incident, and back to the sunpatch and lions.

The apparent jumble is, in fact, not such a jumble. Several active themes make up the emotional context that guides the selection and structuring-on-the-spot process. These themes—aggression-anger, loneliness-sadness, and reconciliation—were activated by the dramatic events of his hitting Tina yesterday and being put in his room. The activated themes select certain events from past and present, elaborate related imaginary events, and assemble all these in a sequence whose logic is guided by the original themes.

Now, Joey starts by viewing the sunpatch. That leads to his experiencing the light, as he has many times since he was six weeks old (chapter 1). He then associates to the lion in the book. The apparent reason for this association is their similar color. The sunpatch experience is also, however, about rising levels of arousal and the self-regulation of his level of excitation. Self-regulation of emotion is partly what he now is struggling with in the context of his anger and sadness, which the lion will come to represent for him. The lion is not yet established as the embodiment of this theme. The theme is still finding itself and filling out.

He then shifts to the lion in the book, which he pictures

to himself, and focuses finally on the lion's teeth. The aggression theme is taking form. He then recalls and "watches" in imagination how his mother imitates a lion. The image of her slow movements retriggers the early but often relived memory of the slow sundance on his wall, which was reactivated just a moment before. He picks up again the image of her lion imitation. Her lion is playful and mild, and the aggression theme is fading. In then saying to himself that his mother is not really a lion, he resuscitates the aggression theme. He goes on to strengthen this theme by selecting the fact that all animals are afraid of lions because they are so strong. At that point, the reinforced theme finds a concrete target which has, in fact, been the guiding context, the motivation, the lingering feeling from last night. Joey relives the scene of hitting the girl and feeling himself seen by other people as dangerous and bad. He re-experiences his feelings of alienation, shame, his being put in his room, his making noise and loud music to express his anger and to comfort himself.

His music recalls another group of early experiences, the feeling of lying in his bed and just watching the world (chapter 2). Perhaps the confinement, the being taken out of action into his room to be a passive observer of a personless world, has played a role in this association. Joey then re-enters the scene of yesterday's events, picking it up at the point of his anger at being confined to his room and throwing his toys around, making like a storm. This, then, activates another piece of the past, well kept alive in memories like his hunger storm (chapter 3). The salient part is not the hunger itself but the feeling upset from within, the pulsations of exploding out and collapsing in. His anger is like that, too. Waves of anger explode out; then, in the momentary quiet that follows, sadness and loneliness rush back to fill him and turn into anger that builds to explode out again, and over again, in waves. That reliving activates more strongly the sadness-loneliness theme, which he then locates upon returning to yesterday's events. Once that theme is ascendant, he returns to the present time and begins to cope with these feelings of sadness by giving them to the lion and then sort of comforting the lion. Here, Joey is using his knowledge of how his mother acts with him, and assumes her role as a comforter. Through this identification with her, he can empathize both with himself and with others.

Joey's experience world is not chaotic, after all. It is a world he is constantly constructing by the give-and-take of selecting life events to attend to, under the influence of a theme or context, and by using whatever events life throws his way to elaborate current themes and design new ones. Joey's lived experience both is guided by themes and seeks to find them. Both processes construct his ongoing experience, so that it is already highly selected and coherent before he reorganizes it into a story.

Joey's story world is a reconstruction of the experience world, itself a construction. This story reconstruction must do many things. First of all, it is of a world made to be observed from the outside by someone else. It is a tale told to another. The experience world, on the other hand, is lived from the inside for no one else. So Joey's first task of reconstruction is to turn the experience world inside-out, so to speak, to fashion the story world. He does this by turning the perceptions and feelings and internal mental states of the experience world into external actions and activities that others can observe on the open stage of the story world. Children, when beginning to tell autobiographical narratives, use mostly action verbs as Joey does: "I played," "he hides," "he moves," "he danced and sang," and so on. And there are far fewer references to feeling states. In Joey's story, there is only one: the lion is "lonely." In his experience world, there are many: the sunpatch "feels good"; his mother is "contented"; animals are "afraid"; and so on.

Joey's next big task of reconstruction is to choose and concentrate the central themes by streamlining and dramatizing them, and doing so in a way that is not too dangerous or embarrassing, or too revealing by making them public. The lion is the perfect vehicle. The lion replaces Joey in the story rendition. The story lion is imbued both with Joey's wishes to be strong and powerful and with his fears of being dangerous and hurtful. The lion commits the actions that are preoccupying Joey: the lion was fighting. And the lion receives the same punishment: being locked in a cage, as Joey was put in his room. In his cage, the lion experiences loneliness and anger, the "big storm," just as Joey did. Joey also knows that his parents discourage aggressiveness in him, and that he must keep it "locked up" behind bars. He has also learned that some experiences are best not shared—not with his parents, anyway. For instance, when in the encounter with his mother over the sunpatch at twenty months (chapter 10), he was lost in the nonverbal sensations and perceptions of the sunshine and was about to touch it with his face, his mother stopped him sharply out of her surprise and disgust. She temporarily shattered Joey's nonverbal world. He then began to realize that guarding, even cultivating, a private world was a necessity for him—and a rewarding one. This knowledge is, perhaps, also responsible for his lion not singing when his parents come in the room. In fact, his lion is generally invisible to all but Joey.

The lion serves yet another function—that of *transitional object,* someone he can be with, and play with, to alleviate the loneliness while he is in his room alone. In the story, the character of Joey is that of the companion-observer to the lion. This assuring role gives him greater distance and control over the loneliness.

The beauty of this disguise is that Joey can express himself through the lion and not be held accountable for what the lion does or feels. After all, the lion is only "pretend." To make this story, Joey has concocted a double piece of magic. First, he created a "pretend" lion and put him at stage center. And, second, he has secretly—from himself, too— imbued the lion with his own qualities. For the story, he has poured himself into two characters, the lion and himself. Joey ends up with a new structure. He has transformed his experience world into a story world.

Joey's story about the pumpkin fish is a good example of this process of transformation. There is something curious about this pumpkin fish. The unlikely combination of pumpkin and fish is just the beginning. This fish is clearly magical: never caught, never seen, it swims like a fish but skips on the surface of the water, too. This fish is somehow related to Joey (he is learning to skip; he "almost caught" it) and to his father (who "maybe even caught one once"). This fish refuses to be caught, to be pinned down, to be looked at closely and classified, or fully understood. Why all the ambiguity and magic? Joey is telling or retelling the story of him and his father and language—of their relationship as known in words.

In the original episode of "Pumpkin" (chapter 9) when he was twenty months old, he for the first time put into words his father's pet name for him, "pumpkin." In that moment he pulled together into the one phrase, "me pump-kin," two different things: how his father views and feels about him, and how he sees and feels about himself viewed that way. It is a magical fusion. It is the beginning of a long line of Joey's development. His father finds Joey lovable and wonderful, and Joey wants to become the way he sees himself in his father's eyes—in his mother's eyes, too. This is one of the more powerful forces in shaping a child's development. His parents love him for who he is, for who he was, and for who they hope he will become. He is coming to appreciate himself in all three perspectives as well. In these curious goings-on between parent and child, Joey is loved for who he is and who he isn't yet. And he appreciates himself for who he is, and also for who he isn't yet but may one day become. That is a magical fish! It is both a fish and not a fish. But it is the prize we are after, even though it is uncatchable. Even if it were to be caught for a moment, it would escape because it cannot be held. It is the point in time where present and future meet in the rush forward. It is the becoming yourself.

Remember that yesterday was a tough day for Joey. He hit a girl and was punished. He suffered a lot. The strains with his parents were mostly resolved last night by the time they put him to bed. But since then, life between them has not yet fully resumed its normal ease. This is the larger determining context for the "pumpkin fish" tale. The over-all theme is the desire for a full reconciliation with his parents. By weaving together this story, Joey is weaving himself and his father back together. The "me pumpkin" experience and the pumpkin-fish tale are narrated celebra-tions of him with his father. That is both their origin in experience and their narrated function as story.

The third part of the morning stories, in the kitchen with his mother, shows other fascinating aspects of a child's story making. A story must have beginning, middle, and end. In "real life" and in the experience world, we expect the sequence of events to follow the order in which they actually happened. In Joey's entry of the experience world, we see this "actual" order; but in his story reconstruction as narrated to me, he almost totally reverses the order.

Here are the two sequences of actions in the order of their occurrence in Joey's two worlds:

| *Joey's Experience World* | *Joey's Story World* |
|---|---|
| They sing the song. | They laugh together. |
| Joey pours cream in her coffee. | Joey surprises her. |
| She turns and sees him. | Joey puts two sugars in her cup. |
| She explodes in delight. | Joey pours cream in her coffee. |
| Joey puts two sugars in her cup. | She turns and sees him. |
| They laugh together. | They sing the song. |

Even though Joey has taken this liberty with the sequential order, roughly the same tale gets communicated. He has simply reversed the beginning and the end and turned things around in the middle.

The dramatic tension in Joey's experience world builds (as in the classical pattern of Greek or Shakespearean tragedy) to the turning point when his mother, realizing that he has poured cream in her coffee, is surprised and "explodes in delight." The dramatic tension then winds down from that climax. There is a second, minor high point when Joey and she see that he knows to put two cubes of sugar in her cup.

Four-year-old children, when learning to tell autobiographical narrations, tend to use the classical pattern less than do older children or adults. These young children prefer to tell a story that, like a Poe or a Maupassant short story, achieves its climax and resolves all in the very last lines. Or, they put the dramatic "punch" up front, and let the rest of the story fill in the details afterward, as Joey has chosen to do for what happened in the kitchen. Thus, he starts high: "At breakfast we laughed and we LAUGHED and *LAUGHED* . . . 'cause it was so funny . . . 'cause I surprised her." Then he provides the particulars of what had happened that was so funny and produced the drama.

The story, however, is not finished after the action is filled in. There is the song, which comes in like an afterthought but which is dramatically too powerful. Why this song? And why this way of incorporating it into the story? Here, again, I must resort to the likely themes that are guiding Joey's reconstructions.

The desire and need for reconciliation with his mother after the event of last evening is as strong as it was with his father. This story is really about the coming back together between him and his mother. The song is the one that they sing each night before Joey goes to sleep. A bedtime song is what the parent gives and the child takes to go alone into sleep. It is a powerful bonding ritual.

Last night, after the upsets of the evening, the bedtime story was not sung. Now, this morning, Joey and his mother repair last night's broken ritual. Singing the song at breakfast enacts their reunion to the full normal state of being with each other. Since, in actual time, the singing together precedes the surprises and laughter of the cream and sugar events, this may be the reason Joey has his high point in the beginning. What really happened was that the strongest emotional dramatic action did happen first, when they sang their song together. That was the coming together. Everything after that—the amusing events with the coffee—replayed their coming back together but on a lower level of dramatic tension and in a lighter spirit. In fact, singing the song and all that implied permitted them to have fun and set the stage for it.

In making the story, Joey has shifted the early high point from the singing to the cream pouring. Although he is historically wrong so far as event sequence goes, he is absolutely right as far as the dramatic-emotional sequence goes. The introduction of the song at a late point in the story and his readiness—in fact, his offer to sing it—creates a second dramatic climax at the end. The song was substituted for in the beginning of the story but appears in the end, anyway. So compelling was its role in the morning that it could not stay hidden.

The song itself is an old French love song. Lovely and mysterious, it is all about being profoundly together. It has been around for several hundred years and has run in and out of the lives and personal stories of countless people. What is important here is that now Joey, too, can reach into his cultural heritage and pull out this magnificent thread to weave into his own account of his personal life. His new ability to tell a narrative has put him into contact with his culture in a way impossible before. In this intimate contact, where he makes that culture part of himself and becomes part of it, he becomes another of its myriad carriers.

And, finally, there is Joey's last statement. His "And then, . . . and then it's now. I'm talking to you," is a clear boundary marker, indicating to me that he has finished his story. Having emerged from the events he was relating, he is returning to the immediate present and wants to bring me along. He notifies me that the past has now caught up with the present. Not only can Joey tell a story, but he is aware that the events in it exist in a different time, the past, and in a different interpersonal space, which one enters and leaves with mutually agreed-upon signs and conventions. He is beginning to be a storyteller, the storyteller of his life. He now has in his own hands the power to interpret and reinterpret his own life. Now that he has control over his own past, he will have much greater control over both his present and future.

And once he has control over his past, he can fashion his own diary, at this point, an oral one. Since he no longer has need of me as a sort of interpreter, I can take my leave. From now on he will be directly talking to you.

# Selected Bibliography

~~~~~~~~~~~~~~~~~~

$\mathcal{S}$INCE this is not an academic book, a complete bibliography of the vast array of books and journal articles on early childhood is not appropriate; thus, I must forgo the pleasure of mentioning directly all those who have contributed to the research for Joey's diary. On the other hand, there is no adequate literature for the interested general public. As a compromise, I have selected a variety of books: some by one author, some jointly edited; some written for a broad spectrum of the field, some highly focused.

I hope that the books listed here, arranged according to the part of the diary whose issues they address, will be but a beginning for the reader who wishes to pursue the study of early childhood. And also that it will give you the means to challenge and refine the diary I have invented here, and to reconstruct a better one for the baby or babies you know.

157

# INTRODUCTION

In this chapter I touch on the revolution in infancy research, how the research is done, and how we know what we think babies know. For a view on these issues, see and compare the chapters on infancy in P. Mussen, ed., *Carmichael's Manual of Child Psychology* (New York: John Wiley, 1970); and in W. Kessen, ed., *Mussen's Handbook of Child Psychology*, vol. I (New York: John Wiley, 1983). These standard texts of developmental psychology help establish the nature of the data base and give glimpses of the revolution in progress.

In explaining how and why I decided to write an "autobiographical" diary, I placed much emphasis on the need and importance for parents or any adult to construct for themselves a version of the baby's inner life. Several books with differing perspectives are relevant here. From the more developmental psychological perspective, Kenneth Kaye, *The Mental and Social Life of Babies* (Chicago: University of Chicago Press, 1982). And from clinical and psychoanalytical perspectives, S. Fraiberg, *Clinical Studies in Infant Mental Health: The First Year of Life* (New York: Basic Books, 1980); and D. Winnicott, *Playing and Reality* (New York: Basic Books, 1971).

Memory is one of the three general and ubiquitous topics that reappear throughout the diary. M. Moscovitch, ed., *Infant Memory* (New York: Plenum Press, 1984), provides many valuable contributions about infants' memorial capacities. From a more theoretical viewpoint, R. C. Shank, *Dynamic Memory: A Theory of Reminding and Learning in*

*Computers and People* (New York: Cambridge University Press, 1982); G. M. Edelman, *The Remembered Present: A Biological Theory of Consciousness* (New York: Basic Books, 1990) and E. Tulving and W. Donaldson, eds., *Organization of Memory* (New York: Academic Press, 1972)—have all influenced me greatly.

A second ubiquitous topic has been an infant's capacity to organize his experience, including its categorization and representation. Here I would point to the classic work of Jean Piaget and the contributions in L. Weiskrantz, ed., *Thought Without Language* (Oxford: Clarendon, 1988); E. Rosch and B. B. Floyd, eds., *Cognition and Categorization* (Hillsdale, N.J.: Lawrence Erlbaum, 1978); and G. Butterworth, ed., *Infancy and Epistemology* (London: Harvester Press, 1981).

For the third such topic, the nature of human infancy in its broader biological and evolutionary context, see M. Hofer, *The Roots of Human Behavior* (San Francisco: W. H. Freeman, 1980); and R. Hind, *Towards Understanding Relationships* (London: Academic Press, 1979).


## I. THE WORLD OF FEELINGS


Emotions in infancy is a growing domain of interest. Some landmark starting points are M. Lewis and L. Rosenblum, eds., *The Development of Affect* (New York: Plenum Press, 1978), and their *The Origins of Fear* (New York: John Wiley, 1974); J. Dunn, *Distress and Comfort* (Cambridge: Harvard University Press, 1976); R. Pluchik and H. Kellerman, eds., *Emotion: Theory, Research and Experience,* vol. II (New York: Academic Press, 1983); J. D. Call, E. Galenson, and R. L. Tyson, eds., *Frontiers of Infant Psychiatry,* vol. II (New York: Basic Books, 1985).

The theoretical work of greatest interest to me here has been S. Tomkins, *Affect, Imagery and Consciousness,* vol. I. *The Positive Affects* (New York: Springer, 1962); and S. Langer, *Mind: An Essay on Human Feeling,* vol. I (Baltimore: Johns Hopkins University Press, 1967).

In this part, reference is also made to how infants look and see, and to how they experience objects in space. Good points of departure would be T. G. R. Bower, *The Perceptual World of the Child* (Cambridge: Harvard University Press, 1976); M. Haith, *Rules That Babies Look By* (Hillsdale, N.J.: Lawrence Erlbaum, 1980); and L. B. Cohen and P. Salapatek, eds., *Infant Perception: From Sensation to Cognition,* vol. II (New York: Academic Press, 1975).

## II. THE IMMEDIATE SOCIAL WORLD

The books listed in this domain concern mostly the special place of the human being as an object of interest to infants, and the nature of the early social interaction between the infant and this special social "object." Most of the following contributions, listed chronologically, are invaluable: M. Lewis and L. Rosenblum, eds., *The Effect of the Infant on Its Caregiver* (New York: John Wiley, 1974); D. Stern, *The First Relationship: Infant and Mother* (Cambridge: Harvard University Press, 1977); H. R. Schaffer, ed., *Studies* in *Mother-Infant Interaction* (New York: Academic Press, 1977); E. Thoman, ed., *Origins of the Infant's Social Responsiveness* (Hillsdale, N.J.: Lawrence Erlbaum, 1978); M. M. Bullowa, ed., *Before Speech: The Beginning of Interpersonal Communication* (New York: Cambridge University Press, 1979); E. Tronick, ed., *Social Interchange in Infancy* (Baltimore: University Park Press, 1982); T. Field and N. Fox, eds., *Social Perception in Infants* (Norwood, N.J.: Ablex, 1986). Concerning the role of autolocomotion in the organization of space, as when Joey is carried by his father, see E. Rovée-Collier, ed., *Advances in Infancy Research* (Norwood, N.J.: Ablex, 1990), especially the article by Bennett Bertenthal and Joseph Campos.

## III. THE WORLD OF MINDSCAPES

There are two main topics here: attachment and intersubjectivity. Concerning attachment, the basic tests are J. Bowlby, *Attachment and Loss,* vol. I (New York: Basic Books, 1969), and vol. II (New York: Basic Books, 1973); and M. D. S. Ainsworth, M. C. Blehar, E. Waters, and S. Wall, *Patterns of Attachment* (Hillsdale, N.J.: Lawrence Erlbaum, 1978). For a more recent update, I. Bretherton and E. Waters, *Growing Points of Attachment Theory and Research. Monographs of the Society for Research in Child Development* (Chicago: University of Chicago Press, 1986).

Concerning intersubjectivity in infants, good starting points are the contributions in M. E. Lamb and L. R. Sherrod, eds., *Infant Social Cognition* (Hillsdale, N.J.: Lawrence Erlbaum, 1981); D. Stern, *The Interpersonal World of the Infant: A View from Psychoanalysis and Developmental Psychology* (New York: Basic Books, 1985); A. Lock, ed., *Action, Gesture and Symbol* (New York: Academic Press, 1978); T. Mischel, ed., *Understanding Other Persons* (Oxford: Blackwell, 1974). A. Sameroff and R. Emde, eds., *Relationship Disturbances in Early Childhood* (New York: Basic Books, 1989), gives a wide clinical perspective on attachment issues.


# IV. THE WORLD OF WORDS


The two chapters in this part concern both the acquisition of language and the impact of language on the infant's experience, as well as the related issue of the infant becoming self-reflective. With regard to self-reflection, good starting points are M. Lewis and J. Brooks-Gunn, *Social Cognition and the Acquisition of Self* (New York: Plenum Press, 1979); and J. Kagan, *The Second Year of Life: The Emergence of Self Awareness* (Cambridge: Harvard University Press, 1981).

For the acquisition of language itself and its (re)organization of the world, see E. Bates, ed., *The Emergence of Symbols: Cognition and Communication in Infancy* (New York: Academic Press, 1979); J. S. Bruner, *Child's Talk: Learning to Use Language* (New York: W. W. Norton, 1983); R. Gollenkoff, ed., *The Transitions from Prelinguistic to Linguistic Communications* (Hillsdale, N.J.: Lawrence Erlbaum, 1983); L. S. Vygotsky, *Thought and Language,* E. Kaufmann and G. Vakar, eds. and trans. (Cambridge: M.I.T. Press, 1962); H. Werner and B. Kaplan, *Symbol Formation: An Organismic Developmental Approach to Language and Expression of Thought* (New York: John Wiley, 1963).

## V. THE WORLD OF STORIES

The construction of narrative is an exploding area of study. The following are landmark contributions to the developmental aspects of narration. In chronological order: W. Chafe, ed., *The Pear Stories* (Norwood, N.J.: Ablex, 1980); C. Peterson and A. McCabe, *Developmental Psycholinguistics: Three Ways of Looking at a Child's Narrative* (New York: Plenum, 1983); K. Nelson, *Event Knowledge: Structure and Function in Development* (Hillsdale, N.J.: Lawrence Erlbaum, 1986); J. S. Bruner, *Actual Minds, Possible Worlds* (Cambridge: Harvard University Press, 1986); K. Nelson, ed., *Narratives from the Crib* (Cambridge: Harvard University Press, 1987).

For a view on narrative in a sociological context, see W. Labov, *Sociolinguistic Patterns* (Philadelphia: University of Pennsylvania Press, 1972). And for a view of narrative in a historical, clinical, and psychoanalytic perspective, see the contributions in W. J. T. Mitchell, *On Narrative* (Chicago: University of Chicago Press, 1981).

# Acknowledgments
———— ✦ ————

$\mathcal{T}$HE richest source for this book has been my own children—Alice, Adrien, Kaia, Maria, and Michael, in order of ascending age and freshest memory. Michael, Maria, and Kaia, now old enough to have read the manuscript, have made invaluable comments from the double knowledge of themselves and their father.

Some of the moments in Joey's diary are based on events in the early life of one or another of my real children. Even more important, as infants, they led me as a parent to compose an unwritten record of who I thought they were and what I imagined them to be experiencing—a record I consulted constantly in my efforts to be a good parent. In a sense, Joey's diary is the sixth I have had to invent.

The other main source of material for this diary comes from the parents and infants with whom I have had the opportunity to collaborate, as either therapist or researcher. I want to acknowledge their pervasive contributions.

# ACKNOWLEDGMENTS

The research base of knowledge about infancy is the keel of this book. The selected bibliography acknowledges the many people who have built this base.

In the actual writing of the diary, I have special debts. Nadia Stern-Bruschweiler has viewed the book from its beginning and at almost every stage. As mother and as child psychiatrist, she has helped to inspire, encourage, and re-shape the book. Roanne Barnett consulted in the final phases with great clarity, good sense, and creativity.

I have come to think of Jo Ann Miller, my editor at Basic Books, as a sort of book magician. Just when Joey's diary seemed to be getting away from me, she always helped it reappear, with sure timing. And Phoebe Hoss, my manu-script editor, I think of as a word and sentence magician, turning dull into bright and dead into living with the flick of a pencil.

I want to thank Hyma Schubert and Virginia Sofios for the preparation of the manuscript.

During the period of writing this book, my research has been supported by Warner Communications, Inc.; Le Fonds National de Recherche Suisse; the MacArthur Foundation; and the Sackler-Lefcourt Center for Child Development.

Geneva, March 1990

Daniel N. Stern, M.D., is Professor of Psychology at the University of Geneva and Adjunct Professor of Psychiatry at Cornell University Medical Center–New York Hospital. He is the author of *The First Relationship* (1977) and *The Interpersonal World of the Infant* (Basic Books, 1985). He is the father of five children, ranging in age from two years to twenty-six years.